POSSIBLE WORLDs
& A SHORT HISTORY OF NIGHT

JOHN MIGHTON

Playwrights Canada Press
Toronto

Playwrights Canada Press is the publishing imprint of
the Playwrights Union of Canada: 54 Wolseley St., 2nd fl.
Toronto, Ontario CANADA M5T 1A5
Tel. (416) 947-0201 Fax. (416) 947-0159

Playwrights Canada Press operates with the generous assistance of
The Canada Council - Writing and Publishing Section, and Theatre Section,
and the Ontario Arts Council.

Front cover photo & title page photo by Michael Cooper.
Edited and designed by Tony Hamill.

Canadian Cataloguing in Publication Data
Mighton, John, 1957-
        Possible world; &, A short history of night
Plays
ISBN 0-88754-479-7
I. Title. II. title: A short history of night.
PS8576.I29P68 1992   C812'.54   C92-094425-6
PR9199.3.M533P68 1992

First edition: September 1992.   Printed and bound in Canada.

For Raegan

AUTHOR'S NOTE

I would like to thank Melanie Joseph, Michael Devine, Don Kugler, and Daniel Brooks for their helpful suggestions.

— *John Mighton*

Possible Worlds was first produced by the Canadian Stage Company, November, 1990, at the St. Lawrence Centre, Toronto, with the following cast, in order of appearance:

WILLIAMS	*Oliver Dennis*
BERKLEY	*Bruce McFee*
GEORGE	*Richard Greenblatt*
JOYCE	*Paula Wing*
PENFIELD	*Daniel Brooks*

Directed by Peter Hinton.
Producer — Gregory Nixon.
Assistant director — Brian Quirt.
Stage manager — Tony Ambrosi.
Set & lighting design by Stephen Droege.
Costumes & props designed by Denyse Karn.
Sound design by Allen Cole and Michel Charbonneau.

Possible Worlds was subsequently produced by Dark Horse Theatre, February, 1992 in Vancouver with the following cast:

WILLIAMS	*Peter LaCroix*
BERKLEY	*Don Thompson*
GEORGE	*Colin Heath*
JOYCE	*Denyse Wilson*
PENFIELD	*Rupert Lindsay*

Directed by Robert Garfat.
Stage manager— Luc Corbeil.
A. S. M. & props — Chris Savage.
Set & lighting design by Rebekah Johnson.
Costume design by Jannette Bijde-Vaate.
Sound design by Earle Peach.

The Characters

GEORGE, *in his Twenties.*

JOYCE, *in her Twenties.*

BERKLEY, *a detective.*

WILLIAMS, *his assistant.*

PENFIELD, *a neurologist.*

The doctor, business people, and other small roles can be doubled. The doubling need not be heavily disguised.

The Setting

A bachelor apartment. Various rooms and offices.

Scene One

The lights rise. Downstage: a body covered by a blood stained sheet. A man sits nearby. A second man enters.

BERKLEY   What have you got for me Williams?

WILLIAMS   Break in, homicide.

BERKLEY   That's the fifth this week. Must be a gang war. They're killng each other off.

WILLIAMS   This one is a little different chief.

BERKLEY   Why? What'd they get?

WILLIAMS   His brain.

Pause.

BERKLEY   What?

WILLIAMS   That's all they took.

BERKLEY   His brain?

BERKLEY *lifts the sheet.*

BERKLEY   Holy shit...what the...

WILLIAMS   He had a thousand dollars in his pocket.

BERKLEY	(*still looking*) Holy shit...
WILLIAMS	Broker. George Barber. We're running a background check...
BERKLEY	Where's the top of his head?
WILLIAMS	Right here chief.

WILLIAMS *produces a plastic bag that holds a piece of skull with some hair on it.*

BERKLEY	What'd they use? A skill saw?
WILLIAMS	There aren't any abrasions.
BERKLEY	Can you get money for a brain?
WILLIAMS	Not that I know of.
BERKLEY	Tell Groves to check all the hospitals... especially the university clinic.
WILLIAMS	Right.
BERKLEY	And get that background check to me as soon as possible.
WILLIAMS	Yes sir. (*turning to leave*) What are you doing?
BERKLEY	Thinking...running over some possibilities.
WILLIAMS	Have fun.

Black.

Scene Two

Lights up. JOYCE *sits reading a paper in a crowded restaurant.* GEORGE *enters with food.*

GEORGE   Do you mind if I sit here?

JOYCE   No, go ahead.

GEORGE *continues to stand.*

GEORGE   (*with great intensity*) There's no place else.

JOYCE   That's fine.

GEORGE *sits.* JOYCE *continues to read.*

GEORGE   Did you see the article about the magnetized baby?

JOYCE   No.

GEORGE   What about those missing brains?

JOYCE   What paper was this in?

GEORGE   *The National Enquirer.*

JOYCE   I don't read *The Enquirer.*

GEORGE	I do...sometimes. For a joke...those guys have some imagination.
	Pause. JOYCE continues to read, trying to ignore him.
GEORGE	I'm George.
JOYCE	Joyce.
GEORGE	I've seen you somewhere before.
JOYCE	I don't think so.
GEORGE	Are you from this city?
JOYCE	I live here, yes.
GEORGE	No, I mean originally.
JOYCE	I grew up in a little northern town. You probably wouldn't have heard of it.
GEORGE	What's it called?
JOYCE	Novar.
GEORGE	Really? I grew up there too.
	Pause.
JOYCE	What part of Novar?
GEORGE	East Lake. Right out near the filling station.
JOYCE	You went to school there?
GEORGE	Sure.
JOYCE	What did you say your name was?
GEORGE	George Barber.
JOYCE	It's funny...I don't remember you.

GEORGE	Well I looked very different back then.
JOYCE	You must have. There were only a hundred people in the high school.
GEORGE	I remember you. You used to swim in the Regatta. You could hold your breath longer than anyone.

Pause.

GEORGE	D'you work around here?
JOYCE	I teach at the University.
GEORGE	Neurology?
JOYCE	That's right. How did you know?
GEORGE	Just a feeling.
JOYCE	What d'you do? Read minds?
GEORGE	I'm a risk analyst.
JOYCE	What's that? Some kind of broker?
GEORGE	No. I advise companies on the risks of investing in various countries.
JOYCE	You must travel alot.
GEORGE	I've been everywhere.
JOYCE	Must be quite a change from Novar.
GEORGE	Oh well...you always miss your roots.

Pause.

GEORGE	You're very beautiful.
JOYCE	Oh please.

GEORGE	You should have been a model.
JOYCE	That's the last thing I'd want to do.
GEORGE	D'you ever think you might have done something different?
JOYCE	No...
GEORGE	Why not?
JOYCE	I'm a fatalist. I think It's pretty silly to wish things were different from what they are.
GEORGE	Oh?
JOYCE	When people see their lives as being different they always make the most trivial changes: if only I'd gone to that party, or taken that job. They never say: if only I'd had two brains or been able to photosynthesize my food. It's as if they think the smaller variations are more likely to have occurred, that God might have overlooked them, but that's just superstition. How could anything be different from what it is?
GEORGE	But surely you've wished you could do things over.
JOYCE	You only have one life — why waste it dreaming about things that could never have happened.
GEORGE	D'you ever fantasize when you make love?
JOYCE	(*laughing*) You got me there...Sometimes. You?
GEORGE	Never. (*tapping his head.*) No brain.

JOYCE *laughs.*

JOYCE	You must meet a lot of women in your travels.
GEORGE	Not really.

JOYCE	I find that hard to believe.
GEORGE	I'm serious. I lead a very Spartan life. I don't believe in promiscuity.
JOYCE	Neither do I. (*standing*) I've got to get back the lab.
GEORGE	How about a show tomorrow night?
JOYCE	I'm working.
GEORGE	What about the weekend?
JOYCE	I'm going to Novar.

Pause.

GEORGE	Maybe I'll see you here again,
JOYCE	I doubt it.

Black.

Scene Three

> GEORGE *sits in a room with several business people. One of them leafs through some papers.*

INTERVIEWER   You used to work for Merrill Lynch?

GEORGE   That's right.

INTERVIEWER   Mr. Parfit recommended you highly. He said you were "uncanny".

GEORGE   Mr. Parfit is a nice man.

> *Pause.*

INTERVIEWER   I'm going to read you some questions. It's something we do with all our applicants. Some of them involve some math you may not be familiar with. Don't worry if you can't get them all.

GEORGE   Thank you.

INTERVIEWER   They were developed by a philosopher at Harvard. Eric Goodman. Does that name ring a bell?

GEORGE   No.

INTERVIEWER   He made a fortune teaching ethics to bankers. Developed the Goodman Theory of Rational Benevolence.

GEORGE   He sounds like a very interesting man.

INTERVIEWER   These questions involve some numbers. You're
                  allowed to use a calculator.

GEORGE   That's alright.

                  Pause.

INTERVIEWER   You can change your mind if you want.

GEORGE   Thank you.

INTERVIEWER   (*reading*) You've been offered an option to buy a
                  hundred and fifty thousand shares of Gentech.
                  Their new treatment for Alzheimer's has been
                  found to cause irreversible hair loss. You stand to
                  make a 60% return at $35.00 a share if they
                  settle the pending law suit out of court. You'll
                  lose a million dollars if they don't. You can pay
                  the vice president half a million dollars to tell
                  you if they've settled. There's a 78.2% chance
                  he'll tell the truth if they've settled and a 49%
                  chance if they haven't. As far as you know there's
                  a 63% chance they've settled. Do you pay the
                  vice president?

GEORGE   No.

INTERVIEWER   Why not?

GEORGE   It's a trick question.

INTERVIEWER   What d'you mean?

GEORGE   Using the numbers you gave me it's worth
                  buying no matter what he says.

                  Pause.

INTERVIEWER   You did the sum in your head?

GEORGE   Yes.

Pause.

INTERVIEWER   The next question is a little more difficult. D'you want some paper?

GEORGE   No.

Pause.

INTERVIEWER   (*reading*) You own a pharmaceutical company. Your staff has just manufactured a new batch of acne pills. Normally they test them by feeding them to a hundred rats and observing how many die. From their previous experience, they have a good idea of how many rats will die if the batch is defective. Unfortunately, due to an irregularity in manufacturing this particular batch...

Lights fade.

Scene Four

GEORGE *is drinking in a crowded bar.*
JOYCE *enters carrying a drink.*

JOYCE   Can I sit here?

GEORGE   Sure.

JOYCE   This place has gotten pretty popular.

GEORGE   Yes.

JOYCE   Five years ago, when I first started selling
stocks, nobody would come here. Too seedy.

Pause.

JOYCE   I saw you coming out of Carson's office this
afternoon. Jumping ship?

GEORGE   Yes.

JOYCE   How'd it go?

GEORGE   Great.

Pause.

JOYCE   I guess you're celebrating.

GEORGE   I guess so.

JOYCE	You don't seem too thrilled.
GEORGE	I'm not.

Pause.

JOYCE	I know you. You used to work for Avery. Why'd you leave? Money?
GEORGE	No.
JOYCE	Sure...Give yourself a few years. You'll be just like everybody.

GEORGE *laughs.*

JOYCE	What's so funny?
GEORGE	I *am* everybody.

Pause.

JOYCE	What's that? Some kind of private joke?
GEORGE	I could have all the money I want.
JOYCE	Couldn't we all.
GEORGE	I know things.
JOYCE	Don't tell me...I've had enough of that kind of information.
GEORGE	This isn't the type of information they can prosecute you for.
JOYCE	Who's your source?
GEORGE	I am.

Pause.

GEORGE	I know everything.

JOYCE	What's my name?
GEORGE	Joyce.

Pause.

JOYCE	That's easy, everyone here knows me. You were staring at me the other night. You spend a lot of time here.
GEORGE	D'you believe in other lives?
JOYCE	Don't tell me. You were once Shirley MacLaine.
GEORGE	No, I mean lives going on right now.
JOYCE	Like being in two places at once?
GEORGE	More than two. A lot more.
JOYCE	You must be a great broker being in hundreds of places at once.
GEORGE	I'm talking about possible worlds. Each of us exists in an infinite number of possible worlds. In one world I'm talking to you right now but your arm is a little to the left, in another world you're interested in that man over there with the glasses, in another, you stood me up two days ago — and that's how I know your name.

Pause.

JOYCE	When did you first realize you were more than one person?
GEORGE	In another life.
JOYCE	Oh?
GEORGE	Seventh grade.
JOYCE	Must have been puberty.

GEORGE   No, it was math.

                JOYCE *laughs.*

GEORGE   I was writing a math test in the seventh grade. I was stuck on the last problem. I could see two ways of doing it but I wasn't sure which would work. Half way through my calculations I suddenly saw myself doing the problem the other way. Only I wasn't just *seeing* myself. For a moment I was actually doing the problem the other way. I looked at my hand and saw a scar. I remembered how I had gotten it. I remembered the dog that had bitten me. Only I'd never been bitten by a dog.

                Pause.

JOYCE   How old are you?

GEORGE   Twenty seven.

JOYCE   How many lovers have you had?

GEORGE   That I can remember?

JOYCE   Yes.

GEORGE   Billions.

                Pause.

JOYCE   Let's go.

                Black.

Scene Five

> *Darkness. Sound of animals in cages.*
> *Lights up on BERKELY and a scientist.*
> *A metal box on the scientist's desk*
> *supports a small glass case. The case is*
> *full of wires and fluid and contains the*
> *brain of a rat.*

SCIENTIST   Would you like to see the animals?

BERKLEY   Yes...Thank you.

SCIENTIST   This is a citation I received for my work on primate nervous systems.

BERKLEY   (*pointing offstage*) What's that?

SCIENTIST   My tank.

BERKLEY   Your tank?

SCIENTIST   My sensory deprivation chamber. I spend a lot of time in there. Not something my colleagues are too keen about...

> *A light flashes on the rat's box.*
> *BERKLEY approaches and examines it.*

BERKLEY   What's this?

SCIENTIST   The brain of a rat.

BERKLEY	Is it alive?
SCIENTIST	Oh yes...Right now it thinks it's pressing a lever for some food. That's why the light flashed. Every time it flashes, we send an electrical impulse to make it think it's been rewarded.

Pause.

BERKLEY	I'm afraid I'm going to have to take this in as evidence.
SCIENTIST	That's alright. I've got dozens of them.
BERKLEY	Dozens?
SCIENTIST	Some biologists think that natural processes create fields of information. I'm seeing if a group of brains, in isolation, can learn something faster after one of them has learned it.
BERKLEY	Are you talking about telepathy?
SCIENTIST	Something like that. The processes of nature are too smooth to be accounted for by purely accidental and mechanical causes.

A monkey screeches.

BERKLEY	D'you have any brains of...larger animals?
SCIENTIST	Like humans?...I read the papers inspector. You think I'm stealing brains.
BERKLEY	We have to investigate every possibility.
SCIENTIST	We're years away from doing this with human brains. We may never be able to do this. Not that the public understands. They'll probably be picketing this place tomorrow.
BERKLEY	Some people might find your research a little frightening.

SCIENTIST   The question is why do we have imaginations? A rat can only imagine so much. It's limited by the structure of it's brain. Creatures like us, that can anticipate possible futures and make contingency plans have an evolutionary advantage. We'd be foolish not to use our imaginations, not to investigate every possible fact.

BERKLEY   What can you use a brain for?

SCIENTIST   Oh, plenty of things. I'm sure you've got some ideas.

BERKLEY   All of the people killed have been very intelligent, in positions of power. I think someone is extracting information from them.

SCIENTIST   Maybe. But there are other possibilities. I think you should consider every possibility...Even aliens.

BERKLEY   Well if you hear from any let me know.

SCIENTIST   You're leaving?

BERKLEY   Yes.

SCIENTIST   Take care of Louise.

BERKLEY   Louise?

SCIENTIST   She's the most intelligent. Her frontal lobes are perfect.

The rat's food light goes on.

SCIENTIST   She's having a snack.

BERKLEY   I'll be in touch.

Black.

Scene Six

JOYCE *is reading in a crowded restaurant.* GEORGE *enters.*

GEORGE   D'you mind if I sit here?

JOYCE *looks at him.*

GEORGE   There's really no place else.

JOYCE   Go ahead.

GEORGE *sits.*

GEORGE   I haven't seen you here in a while.

JOYCE   I've been eating at the lab.

GEORGE   You must be very busy.

JOYCE   (*curtly*) I am.

JOYCE *goes back to her book.*

GEORGE   What d'you do exactly?

JOYCE   I'm looking for ways to increase intelligence.

GEORGE   Maybe you could help me.

JOYCE   I specialize in rat cortexes

> JOYCE *continues reading.*

GEORGE   It must be very interesting.

JOYCE   It's not just that. There's a lot of unnecessary suffering in the world. No political system has ever given people what they want. But neurology will. One day we'll be able to dial and focus our nervous systems the way we adjust our TVs. There will be drugs to extend our lives, increase our intelligence, drugs to erase unpleasant memories. People will look back on the present age with pity. We'll seem like animals to them.

> *Pause.*

GEORGE   How's the dessert?

> JOYCE *laughs.*

GEORGE   What?

JOYCE   A few years ago my life was very complicated. There wasn't a day when I could just relax and forget my responsibilities. So I decided I would try to simplify things. At the cafeteria they served three kinds of dessert: chocolate pudding, a kind of sponge cake, and fruit salad. I decided one day that whenever I was at the counter I wouldn't think. I would always take the fruit salad. I've kept it up ever since — five years.

GEORGE   Don't you think that's a little fanatical?

JOYCE   Probably.

GEORGE   D'you make a lot of resolutions?

JOYCE   All the time.

GEORGE   I remember you at school — always carrying books.

JOYCE   I read all the time. In every book there was
                   always one thing I didn't understand. That would
                   lead me to the next book. I read through whole
                   libraries searching for the secret.

                   GEORGE *laughs.*

JOYCE   You don't say much about yourself.

GEORGE   There's not much to tell. My wife used to say...

JOYCE   Your wife?

GEORGE   She died several years ago...An accident.

JOYCE   I'm sorry.

                   Pause.

GEORGE   It was after she died that I started to travel.

JOYCE   You must have had a very interesting life.

GEORGE   Not really...I usually find myself in a deck chair
                   by the water. I love summer evenings by the
                   water. I like it at dusk when the water has that
                   grey tint that seems to contain every other
                   colour.

                   Pause.

JOYCE   It figures.

GEORGE   What?

JOYCE   That you'd like grey.

GEORGE   I suppose you like black and white.

JOYCE   I've always thought there should be a single clear
                   answer to every question.

GEORGE   Even in love?

JOYCE   Especially in love. I don't trust people who fall
               in love over and over. They're usually the worst
               liars.

GEORGE   You're right. I've never understood people who
               say, "I used to be in love with that person." I
               don't think you ever stop loving. If you do, you
               weren't in love in the first place.

                    JOYCE *looks at her watch and puts
                    some change on the table.*

JOYCE   I've got to get back to the lab.

GEORGE   How about dinner Thursday?

JOYCE   I've got to work late.

GEORGE   If you weren't so busy would you go out with
               me?

JOYCE   If I wasn't so busy I'd be a different person.

                    JOYCE *turns to go.*

GEORGE   Listen, give me a chance. I've never met anyone
               like you, and I've met alot of people.

                    JOYCE *hands him her card.*

JOYCE   Call me.

                    Black.

Scene Seven

> WILLIAMS *sits reading the paper.*
> BERKLEY *enters carrying the apparatus*
> *containing the rat's brain.*

WILLIAMS   Morning chief.

BERKLEY   Morning.

> BERKLEY *puts the box on his desk.*

WILLIAMS   I checked the guy's background. Apparently he
and his wife had a big fight minutes before the
murder — over a present some guy had given
her. She walked out on him.

BERKLEY   Alright...good.

> BERKLEY *sits and starts writing.*

WILLIAMS   Did you see this article in the paper?

BERKLEY   No.

WILLIAMS   It says here that black holes were invented to
confuse Russian scientists...I always thought
there was something fishy about them. What's
that chief?

BERKLEY   (*ironically*) A present for my wife.

> WILLIAMS *examines the apparatus closely.*

WILLIAMS Is it your anniversary?

BERKLEY My what?

WILLIAMS Your anniversary?

> BERKLEY *shakes his head in disbelief, continues working.*

WILLIAMS What does it do?

BERKLEY Do?

WILLIAMS Yeah.

BERKLEY It doesn't do anything.

> *The rat's food light goes on.*

WILLIAMS It's some kind of lamp?

BERKLEY It's not a present. It's the brain of a rat!

WILLIAMS Oh.

> *Pause.* WILLIAMS *examines it.*

WILLIAMS Is it alive?

BERKLEY Yes.

WILLIAMS What d'you suppose it's thinking about right now?

> *Pause.*

WILLIAMS A normal person thinks about sex every two minutes. You think it's the same with rats?

> *Pause.*

WILLIAMS   What if we were in a tank like that? We'd never know it.

BERKLEY   Not you.

WILLIAMS   Maybe someone's making us think whatever they want us to. Maybe that's why all those brains are being stolen! Maybe someone's already stolen ours.

BERKLEY   Why would they want your brain Williams?! What d'you normally think about in the course of a day? Your wife? Your house? Hockey? Why would they want to steal your brain and make you think about hockey all the time? What's the motivation?

                         Pause.

WILLIAMS   You tell me.

                         Pause.

WILLIAMS   Listen, I've been meaning to ask you something.

BERKLEY   What?

WILLIAMS   My wife thinks I should take this course.

BERKLEY   What course?

WILLIAMS   Listen to this. (*reading from a newspaper clipping.*) "The future is here. Join the revolution that does away with dull drills and droning lessons. Increase your creativity and boost your IQ. This course puts you where you belong — on the fast track to superintelligence."

BERKLEY   It couldn't hurt.

WILLIAMS   It has a money back guarantee.

BERKLEY   Good.

WILLIAMS   I'll phone them now.

BERKLEY   What are you going to do when you're more
intelligent Williams?

WILLIAMS   Solve this case.

Scene Eight

A sonata plays. JOCELYN, *played by* JOYCE *with a wig, addresses the audience.*

JOCELYN   Hi. I'm Jocelyn. I'd like to welcome you to the Consciousness Revolution. Over the next few months — if you decide to stay with us beyond this class — I'll be teaching you to use your brains in an entirely new way. You'll learn how to read faster, remember what you learn, create new ideas and coordinate the activity of your right and left hemispheres. Many of you, on graduating, will be able to repeat a thousand phrases from memory after one hearing.

Now at this point some of you may be thinking — that sounds hard. It's been a long day. Perhaps you're saying to yourself — is it worth it? Why should I drag myself here after eight hours of work when I could be at home with someone I love, having a drink, watching TV? For those of you who think that way I have only one question — Why be dumb when you can be smart?

There are a lot of different realities going around today. More new ideas than ever before and they're getting stranger every day. It's not easy to know what to believe, where the truth lies. You have to be smarter than ever to find it. Suppose that rabbits were allowed to reproduce

JOCELYN

(*continued*) without restriction. After two hundred generations the total volume of rabbit would exceed the volume of the observable universe. It's the same with our thoughts. There's only a limited amount of room for them. They have to struggle for survival just like anything else. And only the fittest will survive.

The theme of tonight's session is Imagination. "Imagination rules the world". Does anyone here know who said that? Napoleon said that. He used to go through all his battles in his mind weeks before he fought them. Tonight we're going to do some exercises for our imaginations.

I'd like you to get out the pencils and pads you were given when you came in here tonight. While you're looking for them, I'll draw your attention to the lovely sonata playing over the intercom. Baroque music will be played during all of our sessions because it increases the proportion of alpha waves in the brain. Rock music, which vibrates in the groin, will not be played.

Has everyone found their pencils? Good. We'll start with a visualization exercise which I'd like you to score. As I ask you to imagine things, assign yourself points as follows: 3 points if the image is very clear, 2 points - clear, 1 point - unclear and 0 if you can't imagine anything.

Alright, is everyone ready? You can close your eyes if you want.

See yourself throwing a ball.

Picture the house you grew up in.

Picture a close relative standing in front of you.

Imagine the first few bars of your favorite song.

Is everyone scoring?

Black. The rest of JOCELYN's *instructions are played on a tape in the darkness.*

JOCELYN   Picture the eyes of a close friend.

Feel the hot sun on your skin.

Hear a factory siren.

Feel yourself picking up a heavy object.

Imagine a cold wind when it's raining.

Scene Nine

GEORGE *is asleep in* JOYCE's *couch. She shakes him.*

JOYCE   Hey, wake up. I'm just making some coffee. I hope you don't have anything important to do today. It's ten.

GEORGE   What?

JOYCE   I think Kaufman Brothers can survive the morning without me.

GEORGE   You work for Kaufman Brothers?

JOYCE   What's the matter with you? You weren't *that* drunk last night.

GEORGE   What's that smell?

JOYCE   Coffee. I said I'm making coffee.

GEORGE *holds his head.*

JOYCE   Is something wrong?

GEORGE   My head.

JOYCE   You're hung over.

GEORGE   No.

JOYCE	You want some aspirin?
GEORGE	No, I'm fine. I'm sorry.

> GEORGE *starts dressing. The phone rings.* JOYCE *watches it.*

GEORGE	Aren't you going to answer it?
JOYCE	No, it's probably my office.
GEORGE	What if they fire you?
JOYCE	I hate my job.
GEORGE	Why?
JOYCE	I've never felt comfortable selling things you can't see or touch.

The phone stops.

JOYCE	I guess I'll never know who it was.
GEORGE	What do you sell exactly?
JOYCE	Stocks.
GEORGE	Where were you born?
JOYCE	Right here.
GEORGE	I thought you said Novar....
JOYCE	I think you've got me mixed up with someone else.

Pause.

JOYCE	I'm not usually so aggressive in bars. But you looked so lonely sitting there in the middle of all that activity. The whole world could have disappeared and you would have Just sat there absorbed in your thoughts. I don't think I've ever

JOYCE	(*continued*) seen anyone that looked so alone in my life...Except for some married men I know...You're not married are you?
GEORGE	My wife died three years ago.
JOYCE	I'm sorry.
GEORGE	She was swimming in the ocean and must have gone out too far...

Pause.

GEORGE	D'you ever think things might have been different?
JOYCE	I day dream all the time.
GEORGE	Are you interested in a relationship?
JOYCE	I get restless.
GEORGE	A one-night stand?
JOYCE	I like to forget myself. I love taking chances. I've made a lot of money that way. I could go anywhere, do anything...You shouldn't get involved with me. I'm not very reliable.
GEORGE	There's a moment, when my consciousness shifts...I feel my properties melting, everything I've ever known or felt...nothing holds...it's terrible...but after a few moments I become adjusted...I take on that new life. It's been happening for three years now.
JOYCE	Look that story was funny last night but...
GEORGE	I remember once...I found myself walking down a residential street late at night. There were no trees and a huge moon in the sky. All the houses were made of wood with small windows and phosphorescent geometric flowers painted on the shutters. I was lost. I went up to one of the

GEORGE

(*continued*) houses and knocked. A tall, grey being, shaped like a human but with no nose answered. He wore a short tunic with jewelled medallions and said "Come in will ya?" I noticed there was no furniture.The family was all seated on the floor. I stepped in and they clapped — they had hands — and the tall, grey being rippled as he walked, as if he had no bones. The woman of the house looked like a chicken. When I got within three feet of her she turned around and expanded her backside like a huge rose — she was giving off some sort of scent to welcome me. Standing in the shadows I saw a man I thought I knew. He took my arm and led me out to a field where two men were building with a pile of small rocks.

> *A voice shouts "block" from offstage. The lights fade on* JOYCE, *who remains upstage. A man enters carrying a stone block and sets it down near* GEORGE. *As he exits a second man repeats the action. They continue to fetch blocks from offstage throughout the next scene, occasionally calling "slab" or "block". Their appearnace should suggest victims of a failed experiment. A third man, the guide, played by the scientist, enters and stands beside* GEORGE.

GEORGE   Why are they wearing masks?

GUIDE   Their faces are horribly disfigured.

GEORGE   What are they doing?

GUIDE   Building.

GEORGE   Building what?

GUIDE   I'm not sure.

GEORGE   Why don't you ask them?

GUIDE   They wouldn't understand me.

GEORGE   Why not?

GUIDE   Their language only has three words.

GEORGE   I know two of them.

GUIDE   "Slab" and "Block".

GEORGE   What's the third?

GUIDE   "Hilarious".

GEORGE   That's the word?

GUIDE   Yes.

GEORGE   "Hilarious"? What can they do with that?

GUIDE   Nothing.

GEORGE   How can you have a language with only three words?

GUIDE   Some say they were once an advanced civilization. There was a war. Somehow their memories were selectively destroyed. Only three words survived. Others say they're a very primitive civilization. They learned the first two words by trial and error, and somehow stumbled on the third...a tourist perhaps. Others say they're an ordinary civilization but very concise. It would take fifty encyclopædias to translate the meanings of "slab" and "block" into our language.

GEORGE   What d'you say?

GUIDE   Someone tampered with their brains.

GEORGE   Why?

GUIDE	Just as our bodies move about in physical space, so our minds move about in mental space.
GEORGE	I don't understand.
GUIDE	They're going to kill you. In every world.
GEORGE	But I haven't done anything.
GUIDE	You will.

Lights rise on JOYCE. *The* GUIDE *exits.* JOYCE *stretches as if waking.*

JOYCE	What time is it?
GEORGE	Ten.
JOYCE	How long have you been awake?
GEORGE	Not long.
JOYCE	I don't know what you did to me. I haven't slept like that in years.
GEORGE	Must have been the alcohol.
JOYCE	I wasn't *that* drunk.

Pause.

JOYCE	What's that smell?
GEORGE	Coffee. I'm making coffee.
JOYCE	D'you have any plans for today?
GEORGE	No.
JOYCE	No plans. I've been late at the lab three days this week. And when I'm there I can't concentrate. My colleagues think I've cracked.

GEORGE	(*looking at the blocks by his feet*) Why do you have so many stones in your apartment?
JOYCE	My ex-boyfriend left them. He was a sculptor. He brought them from the sea.
GEORGE	You didn't tell me about him.
JOYCE	We broke up a week before I met you.
GEORGE	Were you in love?
JOYCE	We were going to be married.
GEORGE	What happened?
JOYCE	I found out he was seeing someone else at the same time.

Pause.

JOYCE	When I was at the lab he would bring her here. Now he sends me presents every day. I don't know how someone can lead two different lives.

Pause.

GEORGE	I've never been unfaithful.
JOYCE	How many lovers have you had?
GEORGE	(*holding up his hand*) I could count them on the fingers of one hand.
JOYCE	How many times?
GEORGE	I'm serious. I was married before I was twenty.
JOYCE	(*taking his hand, kissing his fingers*) I love the way you touch me.

They kiss.

JOYCE	Are you thinking about her now?

Pause.

JOYCE   No answer. You're so passive — like smoke — I
                 could put my hand through you. Here — push
                 against me — you see there's nothig there.
                 Maybe that's why you touch me so lightly.

GEORGE   There's a place I'd like to show you.

JOYCE   Where?

GEORGE   Near the ocean. It's very secluded.

JOYCE   I'm sorry — I really can't afford to take time off
                 now.

GEORGE   I think you'd understand me better if you came
                 with me.

JOYCE   I can't. Things are very competitive at work right
                 now.

GEORGE   You'll think more clearly if you have a rest. It
                 will help us both.

JOYCE   You really are trying to ruin me.

GEORGE   We could have everything.

JOYCE   I don't want everything.

GEORGE   Even for a few days.

JOYCE   Alright.

Scene Ten

> JOCELYN's *voice is heard in the darkness.*

JOCELYN Imagine a candle. Those of you who scored less than ten on the visualization exercise should use a real candle.

> *A match flares.*WILLIAMS *lights a candle.*

This will only be necessary for the first few days. After that you should be able to see the bright magic of the flame in your mind's eye simply by closing your eyes and fixing your gaze at a spot in the centre of your forehead...Is your candle lit? Good. Sit three feet away from your real or imaginary candle and relax.

> WILLIAMS *sits.*

The flame is soothing to look at. Focus your attention on it while the specially edited Baroque music plays. (*as music starts*) While your attention is focused attain what Wordsworth called "a happy stillness of mind".

> BERKLEY *enters.*

Now get ready for a journey to the beach.

BERKLEY Surf's up.

WILLIAMS	Oh, hello chief.
JOCELYN	See yourself sitting on a beach in Florida.
	WILLIAMS *turns off the recorder.*
BERKLEY	What are you doing.
WILLIAMS	Just trying to improve myself.
BERKLEY	(*examining the tape.*) By imagining things?
WILLIAMS	It's a good course. Yesterday I learned that we only use a tenth of our brains.
BERKLEY	In your case I'd say that's true.
WILLIAMS	What's the matter with you? You're very irritable. You're not yourself lately.
BERKLEY	It's not me that's changed. When I was young, police work used to be simple. If something was missing you had a good idea why. Not how. But at least why.
WILLIAMS	You've got plenty of leads.
BERKLEY	We don't even know how they cut the skulls! Two of the apartments were locked from the inside. There are murderers running around this city who seem to be able to walk through walls.
	A MAN *enters during* BERKLEY*'s speech and stands behind him.*
MAN	Are you Inspector Berkley?
BERKLEY	(surprised) Yes.
MAN	I'm a friend of George Barber. That is...I was a friend.
BERKLEY	A friend?

MAN	Well, not a friend...an acquaintance. We used to talk sometimes in the hall...about my ideas. I'm the caretaker in his building.
BERKLEY	D'you know anything about his death?
MAN	The night he was murdered I was on the roof. I saw a light.
BERKLEY	A light?
MAN	Yes.
BERKLEY	What sort of light?
MAN	In the sky. As it came closer I saw it was five lights in a row — each about ten feet across.

Pause

BERKLEY	Are you saying you saw flying saucers?
MAN	Yes.

Pause.

MAN	If the Nazis had won World War II we'd be ready. Genetic engineering would have given us the advantage. Now they're stealing our brains.
BERKLEY	Thank you for the information. We'll get back to you.
MAN	There's a world-wide battle for the control of our brains!
BERKLEY	We'll look into it.
MAN	Thank you.

MAN *exits.*

BERKLEY	This morning someone phoned and said they're turning the brains into vitamins.

WILLIAMS	Where are you going?
BERKLEY	I've got a few more leads.
WILLIAMS	You want me to come with you7
BERKLEY	No.
WILLIAMS	Be careful. You don't look so well.

>   BERKLEY *exits.* WILLIAMS *turns on the recorder.*

JOCELYN	Imagine the waves breaking on the hot sand...

Scene Eleven

Lights up on GEORGE, *and* JOYCE
who is examining a photograph.

JOYCE	It's beautiful.
GEORGE	The picture doesn't do it justice.
JOYCE	Why aren't there any people on the beach?
GEORGE	It's not easy to get there. You have to climb out over some rocks.
JOYCE	How did you find it?
GEORGE	My wife used to swim there.

Pause.

JOYCE	You were talking in your sleep last night.
GEORGE	What did I say?
JOYCE	Slab and block. Over and over. I'd say you should come into the lab. I could run some tests. I could probably write a paper on you.
GEORGE	(*looking at his watch*) Shouldn't you be at work?
JOYCE.	No.
GEORGE	What's happened to you?
JOYCE	I've gotten lazy. You've infected me.

GEORGE	I thought you loved your work.
JOYCE	Yesterday there was a demonstration at the lab.
GEORGE	About what?
JOYCE	One of my colleagues. He's keeping an ape's brain alive. I've never seen a crowd so angry. They believe it's in pain.
GEORGE	You should call the police. Those people are fanatics.
JOYCE	Sometimes I wonder what I'm contributing to.
GEORGE	You have a duty.
JOYCE	To use other life?
GEORGE	To investigate every fact.
JOYCE	I work knowing that every idea I have is about to be thought of by someone else. Or already has been. Why should I add one more thought to the pile? There are too many words and most of them outdated. When I was a teenager, I tried to develop a mathematical approach to literature. I invented the meaning decay coefficient.
GEORGE	What's that?
JOYCE	The rate at which a word becomes meaningless over time.
GEORGE	That sounds promising.
JOYCE	I'm not a very good scientist. As a biologist I've seen how everything struggles for more — more food, more protection, more life. But I also know that what you have is always relative to what you can imagine. That's why I try to keep my mind occupied and focused. If I think too much about how things might have been I just get depressed.

GEORGE	You're too strong.
JOYCE	No. I've changed.

Pause.

JOYCE	This morning when I woke up I couldn't remember where I was. I thought I was someplace new...in another time...not the past or future — a place different from any present place. I haven't felt that kind of exhilaration since I was a child. I'd float down at the bottom of the lake watching the sunlight on the rocks, trying to imagine what it would be like to have gills. I knew one breath would let a whole other world in.

Pause.

JOYCE	I wasn't cut out to be a stock broker.
GEORGE	What? What did you say?
JOYCE	I said I wasn't cut out to be a scientist.

Pause.

JOYCE	What's the matter? Are you alright?
GEORGE	I'm fine.
JOYCE	Let's leave tonight. I could use a rest. (*kissing him*)

Scene Twelve

WILLIAMS *stands near a body covered by a blood stained sheet.* BERKLEY *enters.*

BERKLEY What have you got for me Williams?

WILLIAMS Number eleven.

BERKLEY Male or female?

WILLIAMS Female. Nothing missing. Just this... (*pointing to his head*)

BERKLEY *lifts the sheet and looks at the corpse.*

WILLIAMS We searched the whole apartment. No trace of anything. The door was locked from the inside.

BERKLEY This morning I got a call from Twelfth Precinct. They found that caretaker we talked to locked in the freezer of the plant where he worked. He had all the symptoms of having frozen to death...but the freezer wasn't turned on.

WILLIAMS What?

BERKLEY He froze to death at room temperature.

WILLIAMS You think there's a connection to this?

BERKLEY	Yes.
WILLIAMS	What is it?

Pause.

BERKLEY	I've never felt so helpless in my life.

Pause.

WILLIAMS	Looks like rain.

Pause.

WILLIAMS	What are we going to do chief?
BERKLEY	Nothing. Absolutely nothing.

Scene Thirteen

The sound of heavy rain. Lights up on
GEORGE. JOYCE *speaks from off*
stage.

JOYCE   I can't believe this rain. We're going to be washed away. I hope you didn't get too wet.

GEORGE   No.

JOYCE   You must be freezing. I'll put your coat in here so it dries off.

GEORGE   Thanks. (*picking up a bowl and examining it*)

     JOYCE *enters.*

JOYCE   Pretty isn't it?

GEORGE   (*still looking at the bowl*) Yes.

JOYCE   You won't believe who I saw at lunch today.

GEORGE   Who?

JOYCE   Susan Kale. (*pause*) You remember Susan?

GEORGE   No.

JOYCE   I sold her a thousand shares of Gentech this morning. You talked to her for over an hour. The woman who...You haven't heard a word I said.

GEORGE	Sure I have.
JOYCE	What are you doing? You've been staring at that bowl for five minutes.
GEORGE	Comparing it.
JOYCE	To what?
GEORGE	Itself.

Pause.

JOYCE	Don't you need something else?
GEORGE	What?
JOYCE	Well, you see, most people...that is, on this planet...when they compare something, they compare it to a second thing. It's a quaint custom we have.
GEORGE	How d'you know it's only one thing?
JOYCE	Because my ex gave it to me.
GEORGE	I don't follow.
JOYCE	He would never give me two things without pointing both of them out very clearly and going on about how much they both cost. Therefore it's one thing.
GEORGE	But it could have been a lot of things.
JOYCE	Sure, it could have been a beach and we could be sitting on it.
GEORGE	That's what I'm comparing it to.
JOYCE	Right.
GEORGE	I think we should leave tonight.

JOYCE	I don't think so.
GEORGE	Why not? You can afford to take some time off. You're overworked as it is.
JOYCE	It's not work.
GEORGE	What is it?

Pause.

JOYCE	I'm not happy.
GEORGE	What d'you mean...Joyce.
JOYCE	In the beginning, it was all very casual and fun, now all of a sudden you're here every night. It's gotten too claustrophobic.
GEORGE	I can give you more freedom. I won't come over so often.
JOYCE	It's not just that.
GEORGE	What is it?
JOYCE	It's us. When I imagine us together, I like us. We seem perfect for each other. I always think I'm going to enjoy our times together, but as soon as you're here there's always something missing. I've had a lot of fun with you but sometimes when you smile it's aimed a million miles behind me...I never know what's going on inside your head. My friends don't know what to make of you.

Pause.

GEORGE	I heard of someone once who lost his arm in an accident. About three years later he began to feel as if his arm was still there. (*reaching for her*) Sometimes he would reach for things and realize he couldn't pick them up. And the arm was always in pain, a kind of buzzing, stinging pain,

GEORGE   (*continued*) like bubbles exploding in his hand.
                He couldn't predict the pain, he couldn't
                concentrate...sometimes he couldn't finish a
                sentence...and he couldn't believe people didn't
                see how bad the pain was...he expected them to
                see his hand jumping around and pulsating.
                (*sitting down and holding his head*) You can't
                imagine how I feel. For me it's not just an
                arm...I can't tell you...

JOYCE   Look you're not making this very easy...I had a
                carefully rehearsed speech...but now I can't seem
                to remember anything. I'm not doing this very
                well. The point is...I've met someone.

GEORGE   What?

JOYCE   I've been seeing someone for three weeks. I met
                him at work. He's very different from you. I'm
                not saying better — but we have a lot of fun
                together, and he's offered me...more.

GEORGE   More what?

JOYCE   More life.

                        Pause.

JOYCE   D'you want a lift anywhere? It's pouring rain.

GEORGE   No thank you, I...

JOYCE   I'm sorry it had to be this way.

                        Pause.

JOYCE   I didn't have to tell you all this. I could have just
                stopped answering your calls. But I thought it
                would help if you knew what I felt. Next
                time...for your next relationship.

GEORGE   This wasn't a rehearsal...

JOYCE   Please, don't.

GEORGE	You were the only one...in every world...
JOYCE	I'm trying to be rational about this.
GEORGE	My love is infinite.
JOYCE	You'll find someone else. There are plenty of...
GEORGE	They're going to kill me.
JOYCE	Who?
GEORGE	Joyce, please...
JOYCE	Look, you're scaring me. If you don't get out, I'll call the police. (*picking up the telephone*) I'm warning you.
GEORGE	No don't.
JOYCE	Get out!

JOYCE *dials.* GEORGE *moves towards her.*
Black.

Scene Fourteen

	The telephone rings. BERKLEY *sits staring into space. The phone stops.* WILLIAMS *enters.*
WILLIAMS	What's the matter chief? You didn't answer the phone. You've been sitting there for days. You haven't moved from that chair for three days!
BERKLEY	(*to himself*) A rat can only imagine so much...
WILLIAMS	What? What's that?
BERKLEY	Suppose a rat had an enemy...
WILLIAMS	What kind of enemy chief? Another rat?
BERKLEY	No. Like us.
WILLIAMS	Like us?
BERKLEY	(*looking at the brain of the rat*) There's no way the rat could foresee what it's enemy was going to do, because it couldn't even imagine it...
WILLIAMS	Unless it was a very smart rat.
BERKLEY	No, Williams, it's limited by the structure of it's brain. It can't even form the right kind of thoughts.
WILLIAMS	Oh.

BERKLEY   And we're up against the same kind of enemy.

                 Pause.

WILLIAMS   So what do we do?

BERKLEY   Nothing. There's nothing we can do. We're
                 fucked.

WILLIAMS   Oh.

BERKLEY   We'll just have to hope that whatever it is leaves
                 us in peace. (*pause*) We're nothing, Williams, in
                 the scheme of things.

WILLIAMS   Oh I wouldn't go that far...

BERKLEY   This morning I stood in the middle of the street,
                 just stood there and watched the traffic...

WILLIAMS   That's not like you chief.

BERKLEY   I stood in the middle of the street and people
                 swept by me like I wasn't there. I felt like a
                 ghost. I've got a few more cases to solve and
                 then I'm going to retire and die. What kind of life
                 is that?

WILLIAMS   The pension's not bad.

BERKLEY   I still remember something that scientist said. He
                 said to me — Do you think the numbers didn't
                 exist before we humans found them? Do you
                 think the number two didn't exist? Every thought
                 you can think, officer, existed before you did.
                 And those thoughts affect us. The possibilities
                 swarm around us...Sometimes you can almost
                 see them. They...

                 As BERKLEY *speaks,* WILLIAMS
                 *rolls up some paper and circles around
                 the desk. He swats at something.*

WILLIAMS   Aha!

BERKLEY	What are you doing Williams?
WILLIAMS	This brain seems to be attracting flies. I think it's leaking. It smells awful. Look at that...it's light went on.

The light blinks on a few more times.

WILLIAMS	What's happening? 1 think it's trying to signal us.
BERKLEY	Don't be ridiculous. It's hungry. It's trying to get food.
WILLIAMS	How can we help it?
BERKLEY	We can't.
WILLIAMS	I can't stand it!
BERKLEY	It's not real Williams. It's not really hungry.
WILLIAMS	But it thinks it is.

Pause. The light blinks on.

BERKLEY	(*upset*) Look, I've got other cases. I don't have all day to hang around here. I'll see you later.
WILLIAMS	Right chief.

BERKLEY *exits.*

WILLIAMS	I'm sorry. There's nothing I can do. (*pause*) I don't know how to help you. (*pause*) But there's someone who does. (*picking up the box.*)

Black.

Scene Fifteen

Sound of waves. JOYCE *sits in a deck chair reading.* GEORGE *enters and sits beside her.*

GEORGE   It's a beautiful view, isn't it?

JOYCE   Yes.

GEORGE   Have you been in swimming?

JOYCE   Yes. The water's lovely. (*going back to her book*)

GEORGE   Are you a good swimmer?

JOYCE   (*a little surprised*) Well, yes...I suppose so...

GEORGE   I love this time of evening. When the water seems to contain every colour.

            JOYCE *goes back to her book.*

GEORGE   How've you been keeping Joyce?

JOYCE   How do you know my name?

            Pause.

GEORGE   There was a time...quite a few years ago...

JOYCE   You do look familiar. I've forgotten your name.

GEORGE	George.
JOYCE	George! Yes of course. George...
GEORGE	Barber.
JOYCE	George Barber! Of course. We were at Cambridge together in '83.
GEORGE	No.
JOYCE	You weren't at Cambridge?
GEORGE	No.
JOYCE	You owned a clothing store on Church Street!
GEORGE	No.
JOYCE	You're keeping me in suspense. How do I know you?
GEORGE	We used to live together. We were married once.

Pause.

JOYCE	I think you're mistaken.
GEORGE	I wouldn't forget a thing like that.

JOYCE *moves to stand up.*

GEORGE	No, please, don't go...Are you still studying the brain?
JOYCE	Yes.
GEORGE	Dating anyone?
JOYCE	Yes, in fact he's here right...
GEORGE	Found a way to increase intelligence?

JOYCE	How d'you know so much about me? Who set this up? Did Bob...
GEORGE	It's not a joke.
JOYCE	I don't know you.
GEORGE	I've always been interested in the brain. I heard an interesting story once. A neurotic young man asked a psychologist how he could find peace of mind. "How can you lack anything," said the psychologist, pointing to his head, "when you possess the greatest treasure in the universe?"
JOYCE	Well that's a very interesting story, but I'm afraid I have to go.
GEORGE	Please don't.
JOYCE	I'm afraid you have me mixed up with someone else.
GEORGE	Turn around.
JOYCE	No.
GEORGE	Turn around.(*turning her*)
JOYCE	Let go of me!
GEORGE	You see, you have a mole on your shoulder. I'm not insane.
JOYCE	Let go! Help!
	GEORGE *puts his hand over her mouth.*
GEORGE	I'm not going to hurt you Joyce. I love you. I've always loved you.
	A man enters. JOYCE *escapes by biting* GEORGE's *hand.*

MAN   Hey!

> GEORGE *runs off.*

MAN   What happened?

JOYCE   I don't know. That man said he knew me.

MAN   Come back to the hotel. I'll call the police. We
               should have stayed at home.

Scene Sixteen

GEORGE *is sitting in an office being questioned by a doctor, played by* PENFIELD.

GEORGE I can hardly say I have a memory, Doctor.

DOCTOR Why not?

GEORGE It would be more accurate to say in the collection of people I call me, a memory occurs.

DOCTOR Do you believe in the soul?

GEORGE I used to think there was something extra... something that went along with all the changes, but now I don't think so.

DOCTOR Why did you attack that woman?

Pause.

GEORGE I don't know. I lost control...I regret it.

DOCTOR What do your other selves think about it?

GEORGE Most of them don't know about it.

DOCTOR Oh?

GEORGE

When I believed I had a soul I was imprisoned in myself. I felt I had to be consistent among my lives. But now I realize they're all different and I can enjoy them all. If there's a unity that makes them all me, I don't know what it is. This is simply a world where I happen to be a criminal. It's not very important. Have you ever imagined killing someone? It's about as important as that. There are so many worlds.

GEORGE *starts to cry.*

GEORGE

Sometimes when I'm falling asleep, I think I'm floating in the sea...two inches below the surface...rocking in the warm salt water like someone who's drowned. Above me the sky is full of clouds, but they're hard-edged like glass. The whole sky glitters like glass. I close my eyes and hear voices and when I open them again I'm surrounded by a net of branches that grow right into my skin.

Water starts to run down the walls of the room.

DOCTOR

I'm afraid we're going to have to keep you here for a little while, under observation.

GEORGE

That's alright. I have nowhere to go.

DOCTOR

You could go anywhere if you really wanted.

GEORGE

No.

Pause.

GEORGE

I know where I am now. There's only one world. I've been dreaming.

Pause.

GEORGE

I'm in a case.

Scene Seventeen

Sound of the ocean. BERKLEY *works at his desk.* WILLIAMS *enters.*

WILLIAMS   Morning chief.

BERKLEY   Morning.

WILLIAMS   You have a good weekend?

BERKLEY   Yes. I went away to the beach with my wife. I feel like a new man.

WILLIAMS   You want me to get you some coffee?

BERKLEY   Sure. That would be great.

Pause.

WILLIAMS   By the way...those brains we were looking for...

BERKLEY   Yes.

WILLIAMS   I found them.

Pause.

WILLIAMS   I went to see that scientist, Penfield — took back the rat's brain. He had a bunch of human brains locked up in a cupboard. Hooked up to lights just like that rat. Here's my report.

BERKLEY	(*taking the report*) Thank you.
WILLIAMS	I asked Mrs. Barber, the wife of the...brain that was married to come down. She's here now. You want to talk to her?
BERKLEY	Yes. Thank you.

WILLIAMS *turns to exit.*

BERKLEY	Good work Williams.
WILLIAMS	Thanks chief.

WILLIAMS *exits.* BERKLEY *reads the* report. WILLIAMS *enters with* JOYCE.

WILLIAMS	In here.
JOYCE	Thank you.

WILLIAMS *exits.*

JOYCE	I understand you found the man who killed my husband.
BERKLEY	Yes.
JOYCE	That's something I suppose....But it won't bring him back to life.
BERKLEY	He's still alive.

Pause.

BERKLEY	We found his brain...in a cupboard...hooked up to a life-support system. According to Dr. Penfield, he won't survive more than a few weeks.

Pause.

BERKLEY   He's floating in an aquarium supported by wires. He's downstairs if you'd like to see him.

JOYCE   No thank you.

            Pause.

JOYCE   I was just getting adjusted to his death...it's hard...we were married before we were twenty. I was the fifth girl he'd gone out with. We were very happy. He was going to leave his job at the market for me. I was going to give up my research to travel around the world with him. He was the most important thing in the world. He meant everything to me...There's so much we didn't do.

BERKLEY   What would you like me to do with the brain when it stops...functioning?

JOYCE   Donate it to science.

BERKLEY   What?

JOYCE   It was a joke inspector.

            Pause.

JOYCE   I'll bury it in Novar with the body.

            Pause.

JOYCE   Is he in pain?

BERKLEY   Dr. Penfield says he was never able to get more than a rudimentary consciousness going. There's a light that flashes occasionally, but we don't know what it means. Your husband probably isn't aware of who he is. Penfield described it as a kind of fluctuating dream state. Very discontinuous.

            Pause.

JOYCE   If I hadn't left him alone that day...it would never
               have happened.

BERKLEY   You can't blame yourself.

JOYCE   We fought over the stupidest thing. A man at
               work had given me a present.

                         Pause.

BERKLEY   If there's anything I can do to help...

JOYCE   No.

                         Pause.

JOYCE   The hardest thing is knowing he's alone...D'you
               think he remembers me? He once said that every
               second thought was about me.

BERKLEY   I'm sure he's thinking about you somehow...

Scene Eighteen

Sound of the ocean, distorted, as if contained within a layer of glass. Lights up on JOYCE *and* GEORGE. JOYCE *carries a sheet.*

JOYCE   Careful, it's wet here.

GEORGE   I'm alright.

JOYCE   (*holding him*) You're soaking. That was quite a fall. You could have broken your arm.

GEORGE   I'm fine.

JOYCE   (*touching the ground*) The sand's a bit damp here. Good thing I brought a sheet.

           JOYCE *spreads the sheet and sits.* GEORGE *picks up a rock.*

GEORGE   There must be a thousand fossils in these rocks. So many failed ideas. (*taking a deep breath*) You can smell the waste here.

           GEORGE *sits beside* JOYCE.

JOYCE   Tomorrow, if it's nice, we'll go swimming.

GEORGE   Sure.

GEORGE *kisses* JOYCE.

JOYCE   You're so happy today.

GEORGE   It's nice to be off work.

JOYCE   I'm glad we decided to come here.

GEORGE   I knew you'd like it here— it's one of my favorite spots.

Pause.

JOYCE   It's strange.

GEORGE   What?

JOYCE   Why are we the only ones on the beach?

GEORGE   It's late.

Pause.

JOYCE   It's beautiful here.

GEORGE   It's heaven.

JOYCE   You've been there too?

GEORGE   Oh yes.

JOYCE   What's it like?

GEORGE   Heaven is very strange. I'd go there again but I'd pack differently.

Pause.

JOYCE   I've always wondered why we have imaginations. One day I'll write a paper. When I was a little girl I used to think it was a different world I saw under the water.

GEORGE   What kind of world?

JOYCE	I really can't put it into words.
GEORGE	Try.
JOYCE	I can't.

Pause.

JOYCE	The word "not" is really magical. I could describe something and say — "But it's *not* that, it's something more" — and you'd know what I meant. It's a way of getting around our ignorance. That's how they used to describe God. Everything we can't conceive of. We say "Things might not have been the way they are", and feel free or uneasy. But there's really nothing behind it. Just a bunch of ghostly possibilities. Because in the end, everything simply is.

Pause.

JOYCE	How's your arm?
GEORGE	Fine.
JOYCE	(*taking his hand*) You have the most beautiful fingers. They're so soft. (*kissing each of his fingers*) One for each of your lovers. (*pause*) It's almost dark. Soon there'll be stars. We'll have to make a wish.
GEORGE	I thought you didn't wish.
JOYCE	Only for what's possible.
GEORGE	Does that include me?
JOYCE	Yes. I couldn't ask for more.

They kiss.

JOYCE	Look...What's that light?
GEORGE	Where?

JOYCE	Out there...blinking on and off.
GEORGE	It's a buoy to warn the ships.
JOYCE	There couldn't be shoals that far out.
GEORGE	Why not...
JOYCE	No, look...that flash was longer. (*standing*) Someone's signaling us.
GEORGE	Are you sure?
JOYCE	What should we do?
GEORGE	I don't know. We're miles from a phone.
JOYCE	Someone could be drowning out there...What should we do?
GEORGE	I don't know!

Pause.

JOYCE	It's stopped.
GEORGE	Thank God.... Whatever it was, there's nothing we can do about it. The coast guard will see it.

Pause.

JOYCE	I'm cold.
GEORGE	Sit down. I'll hold you.
JOYCE	(*sitting beside him*) We should go back soon.
GEORGE	Yes.

Pause.

GEORGE	We'll go away for a year.
JOYCE	A year?

GEORGE   Yes. We'll keep moving. We'll never be alone. We don't want to be sixty, regretting all the things we never did.

Pause.

JOYCE   Where will we go?

GEORGE   Everywhere.

They lie down and hold each other. The lights fade. Far away, in the darkness, a small light blinks on and off several times.

The End.

A SHORT HISTORY OF NIGHT

JOHN MIGHTON

Title page photo: Guillermo Verdecchia (back left), David Hewlitt (back right), Clifford Saunders (foreground), and John Gilbert (centre) in the Crow's Theatre production of A Short History of Night, May, 1991, The Poor Alex Theatre, Toronto. *Photo by Michael Cooper.*

Author's Note

When people think about the future, they tend to imagine a world in which, for better or worse, everyone agrees. In dystopias like Huxley's Brave New World the agreement is imposed from above; in utopias it is spontaneous and based on truth. But if the human mind is incapable of understanding the world in its entirety, then people may never entirely agree. Perhaps we should start preparing for a future in which people don't agree, in which tolerance will have to be the chief virtue.

— John Mighton

Foreword

The play is based on the lives of two 16th Century scientists: Johannes Kepler, who discovered the first planetary laws of motion and prepared the way for Isaac Newton, and Tycho Brahe, the great Danish astronomer. Some of the material has been taken from Kepler's diaries (excerpted from Arthur Koestler's The Sleepwalkers) and from accounts of the wars and witchcraft trials of the time. The dates and substance of some events have been changed — for instance, it was Kepler's mother, not his wife who was tried and almost executed for witchcraft. Several speeches are based on ideas of René Descartes (Act One, Scene Seven) Galileo Galilei (Act One, Scene Seven), and Marcus Aurelius (Act Two, Scene Three).

A Short History of Night was first produced by Dark Horse Theatre, May, 1990, Vancouver with the following cast:

JEPP	*David Garfinkle*
REMY & INFECTED MAN	*Peter Giaschi*
FATHER, BRUNO, & SOLDIER	*Keith Martin Gordey*
LONGOMONTANUS & URSUS	*Tim Healy*
MOTHER, MARGARET, & BARBARA	*Sharon Heath*
EISLER, MAN ON HILL, & SOLDIER	*David Hurtubise*
TYCHO BRAHE	*Ian McDonald*
JOHANNES KEPLER	*Mitch Molloy*

Directed by David Wilson.
Stage Manager — Kara Elliott.
Production Manager — Jan Werger.
Set & lighting design by Mark Deggan.
Original sound design by Earl Peach.
Costume design by Terri Bardon.

A Short History of Night was produced by Crow's Theatre, May, 1991, at The Poor Alex Theatre, Toronto, with the following cast, in order of appearance:

EISLER, THOMAS	*Oliver Dennis*
TYCHO BRAHE	*John Gilbert*
REMY, BRUNO	*David Hewlett*
JEPP THE DWARF	*Clifford Saunders*
JOHANNES KEPLER	*Michael Simpson*
BARBARA, MARGARET, MOTHER	*Jane Spidell*
LONGOMONTANUS, FATHER	*Guillermo Verdecchia*

Directed by Jim Millan.
Associate director — Sue Miner.
Original score by Lesley Barber.
Set & lighting design by Glenn Davidson.
Costume design by Carole Griffin.
Stage manager — Maria Popoff.

The Characters

JOHANNES KEPLER	*An astronomer.*
TYCHO BRAHE	*An astronomer, twenty five years Kepler's senior.*
BARBARA	*Kepler's wife.*
JEPP	*A dwarf, credited with second sight.*
LONGOMONTANUS	*An astronomer, jealous of Kepler.*
REMY	*An intellectual prodigy of 19 years, and officer of the Inquisition.*
BRUNO	*An astronomer.*
EISLER	*A doctor.*

Other small roles can be doubled — BRUNO can be doubled with REMY.

The Setting

A castle and locations nearby in Bohemia. Late 16th Century

Act One, Scene One

KEPLER *addresses the audience.*

KEPLER   The day I was born my father was away at war. It was six months before he received the news. He came on horseback, in a cold season, through a country devastated by war.

Several beams of anlged light fall on a cradle, centre stage.

KEPLER   The soul leaves the stars and enters the body at the moment of birth. The planets, the angles at which they subdivide the sphere, that's what determines our fate. Our souls react to those angles, the harmonic proportions of the light rays as they strike the earth.

A shout is heard from offstage.
KEPLER's FATHER stumbles on dressed.as a soldier. His MOTHER follows. Lights out on KEPLER ,

FATHER   Where is he? Where's Johannes?

MOTHER   It's late. You'll wake him.

FATHER   I'm not making any noise.

MOTHER   Sh!

FATHER   He needs to learn.

FATHER *grabs the cradle.* MOTHER *struggles with him.*

MOTHER   Let go. You'll drop him! He's falling!

FATHER   Get away! (*pushing her away, shouting into the cradle*) I'm back! D'you hear me? I'm back! We had a great victory. They fought like fiends but we beat them! Do you hear me? We beat them!

                Pause.

FATHER   What's the matter? He's not crying.

MOTHER   He never cries.

FATHER   It's me — your father!....Don't you recognize me? I'm going to teach you to fight. You were born at the right time. King Frederick. The Hapsburgs. The Turks. They're all looking for men! You'll have the good fortune to witness a revival in the long-lost art of war!

                Pause.

FATHER   He's staring at me.

MOTHER   Let him sleep.

FATHER   HEY!...He didn't even blink. What's happened to him?

MOTHER   Nothing.

FATHER   He's dead.

MOTHER   Don't be a fool. His eyes are open.

FATHER   His skin is white. It's as cold as death.

MOTHER   It's cold tonight.

FATHER   What have you done to him?

MOTHER	Nothing.
FATHER	Witch! What have you fed him? He's in a trance.
MOTHER	He's only a baby. How can you be so afraid?

FATHER *takes out a dagger.*

FATHER	(*to the cradle*) I've brought you something. A little sword. I cut it from the belt of a Spaniard.

FATHER *puts the dagger into the cradle.*

MOTHER	He'll cut himself.

MOTHER *tries to take the cradle.*
FATHER *pushes her down.*

FATHER	I'll teach you to fight. For God! That's why we were created. If I had one foot in heaven I'd pull it out again — to go to war!

Act One, Scene Two

> TYCHO BRAHE *and another man stand looking at the sky.*

BRAHE   Look. There. Now do you see it?

MAN   Yes.

BRAHE   I'm not dreaming?

MAN   No.

BRAHE   Has it moved?

MAN   No.

> *Pause.*

BRAHE   Hallelujah!

MAN   We're drunk.

BRAHE   It hasn't affected my eyes.

MAN   I'll call Ursus...Ursus!

BRAHE   Why call that imbecile? Can't you see it with your own eyes?

MAN   Perhaps it's a subluniary body....a comet.

BRAHE   It hasn't moved.

MAN	It's very unusual.
	URSUS *enters.*
MAN	Look up there, in the centre of Cassioppeia. Do you see a light?
URSUS	Yes.
MAN	Brighter than the rest?
URSUS	Yes.
BRAHE	It's a new star.
URSUS	What? You're mad. The heavens are immutable.
MAN	Perhaps it's the second coming.
URSUS	It's a comet.
BRAHE	It's not moving.
URSUS	Very slowly...
BRAHE	Trash!
URSUS	...Or coming towards us.
MAN	There will be plagues and famines.
BRAHE	Where's its tail?
URSUS	It's a tailless comet. I've discovered a tailless comet!
BRAHE	Moron! It's a star! A new star. Tycho's star. I discovered it. I've proven the heavens can change. Aristotle was wrong! I'll be the talk of Europe. More famous than Copernicus. D'you see these rags gentlemen? Tomorrow I'll be rich.
	Pause.
URSUS	It moved.

BRAHE   Bastard! (*drawing his sword*)

MAN   You can't duel here. It's too dark.

          URSUS *draws his sword.*

MAN   Gentlemen, please. You're drunk.

          URSUS *lunges at* BRAHE *and cuts off
          his nose..* BRAHE *screams and falls to
          the ground.*

MAN   You've cut off his nose!

Act One, Scene Three

Lights up on KEPLER.

KEPLER   I cannot say I have always been strong. At the
age of four I almost died of small pox. I was in
very ill health and my hands were affected.
Throughout adolescence I suffered continually
from skin ailments. At fifteen I developed scabs
and chronic putrid wounds on my feet which
healed badly. On the middle finger of my right
hand I had a worm, on the left a huge sore. The
mange took hold of me. Then there was the dry
disease. At Cupinga's I was offered union with a
virgin. On New Year's Eve, 1591, I achieved this
with the greatest possible difficulty, experiencing
the most acute pains of the bladder. (*pause*) I
predicted a comet that year and was accompanied
by the former virgin to a high place to see it. We
sought a sheltered spot and watched for the comet
as Venus entered the second house.

Lights up on BARBARA *sitting
nearby.*

BARBARA   How's your Aunt Kunigard?

KEPLER   Dead.

BARBARA   Katherine?

KEPLER   She too is dead.

BARBARA	Sebaldus?
KEPLER	She was skillful and intelligent, but married most unfortunately, lived sumptuously, squandered her goods and is now a beggar.

Pause.

BARBARA	How's your father? He was always nice to me.
KEPLER	Saturn in seven made him study gunnery. He had many enemies and ran the risk of hanging. So he fought in Holland. A jar of gunpowder burst and lacerated his face. He's in exile.

KEPLER *takes out a knife.*

KEPLER	This is all he left me.
BARBARA	You've had a difficult life.
KEPLER	I take comfort in the stars. When the storm threatens us with shipwreck, we can do nothing more noble than fix the anchor of our studies into the ground of eternity.

Pause.

KEPLER	God has chosen me to receive the insight of the creation plan.

Pause.

BARBARA	You're very young.
KEPLER	Nineteen.
BARBARA	And God told you this?
KEPLER	Yes.
BARBARA	In a dream?
KEPLER	No. In a mathematical proof.

Pause.

BARBARA	Are you hard working?
KEPLER	To excess.
BARBARA	Do you expect riches?
KEPLER	No.
BARBARA	Love?
KEPLER	No.
BARBARA	Fame.
KEPLER	I expect nothing of that sort.
BARBARA	You don't seem very happy.
KEPLER	I don't look for such happiness as the foolish lovers of the world experience, but such as the good and faithful servants of Christ wait for. All human consolation is in vain.

Pause.

BARBARA	You should have joined the ministry.
KEPLER	I tried. They wouldn't let me.
BARBARA	Why not?
KEPLER	They said I am too opinionated.
BARBARA	How unfair.
KEPLER	I have often incensed my school fellows against me. Once, out of fear, I was driven to betray them. I argue with men of every profession for the profit of my mind. I am like a dog worrying a bone — I cannot help gnawing. I hate many people exceedingly and avoid them.

Pause.

BARBARA   Come and sit down. It's a beautiful evening.
                 Look at the stars.

                          KEPLER *sits beside her.*

BARBARA   What's that one called?

KEPLER   Where?

BARBARA   The little one. Beside the North Star. I've often
                 watched it.

KEPLER   I cannot see. My eyes are weak.

BARBARA   (*laughing*) A nearsighted astronomer.

KEPLER   I see with the eye of my mind.

                          Pause.

BARBARA   I'm sorry you're so unhappy. I like you . My
                 father likes you. You should visit us some time.
                 I have a wonderful family and I would do
                 anything to please them. Especially my father.
                 He's always singing. When I was a child he used
                 to throw me up in the air and catch me. He said
                 he'd throw me right up into heaven. ....How far
                 is heaven?

KEPLER   Two thousand four hundred and fifty million
                 miles.

BARBARA   How did you figure that out?

KEPLER   There are five perfect bodies that can be inscribed
                 between the earth and the five planets. The
                 tetrahedron, the hexahedron, the octahedron, the
                 dodecahedron and the isocahedron. God loves
                 Geometry.I deduced it from their dimensions.

                          Pause. BARBARA *takes his hand.*
BARBARA   We're alone here.

KEPLER   Yes.

BARBARA	Did you like it?
KEPLER	Like what?
BARBARA	Don't be coy.
KEPLER	It was necessary.

Pause.

BARBARA	It's late. I'm cold. Where's your comet?
KEPLER	I can hardly predict it to the minute.
BARBARA	I can't stay much longer. My father is expecting me.
KEPLER	Alright.
BARBARA	We'll see each other tomorrow?
KEPLER	Yes. I'll bring your father's horoscope.

Pause.

BARBARA	My father has known your family for some time. He's appalled by your poverty, but recognizes your promise as an astrologer.

Pause.

BARBARA	I like you. We've known each other for three months. You seem noble and trustworthy, which is rare. Your features aren't unpleasing. And we share the same faith....If you asked me to marry you, I wouldn't refuse.
KEPLER	You'd have me?
BARBARA	I could do worse.
KEPLER	I have to consult my charts.

BARBARA   Alright. But don't keep me waiting too long. I
                   have plenty of prospects.

KEPLER   I won't.

                   BARBARA *exits.* KEPLER *looks at
                   the sky.*

Act One, Scene Four

Sounds of war. A man enters and stands looking at the sky. He shouts "Help me!" several times. KEPLER and BARBARA enter. She is pregnant.

BARBARA   Look — can you see it now?

KEPLER   Yes, that's it. That's the castle.

BARBARA   Thank God! We're saved.

KEPLER   We should rest here.

BARBARA   Is it safe?

KEPLER   I can't go any further. My feet are bleeding. This morning I discovered a small cross on my left foot. In the very place where Christ was pierced.

KEPLER sits and pulls off his boot.

KEPLER   Yesterday the heat afflicted me and constricted my bowels. Now the gall has gone to my head. I think I am one of those people whose gall bladder has a direct opening on the stomach. Such people are short lived as a rule...What has happened to the trees?

BARBARA   It must be the scorching wind.

KEPLER   Or the worms...this country is diseased.

Pause.

KEPLER   (*pointing to his foot*) Look. Can you see it?

BARBARA   (*looking closely*) Yes.

KEPLER   You know I am not weak.

BARBARA   Yes.

KEPLER   I have endured pain that would have killed ten men. I have worked without rest these five years.

BARBARA   I know...Can you walk?

KEPLER   The world is overrun by fanatics. No one knows what to believe. In Silesia a whole village was put to the stake. I should have become a soldier like my father. They have taken everything from us....It was a mistake to marry me. I foresaw it. In predicting disaster I am usually right.

BARBARA   God must have intended it in making me pregnant...Don't give up. Your friend is our hope.

KEPLER   Yes. In that castle the greatest minds of Europe are gathered. Kings and great nobles flock there to learn about the stars. One of his instruments alone is worth a hundred salaries at the university. I've sent him my theory of the planets. He'll welcome us with open arms.

BARBARA   Can you walk? We should go.

KEPLER   Yes, I feel my life returning.

They begin to exit.

BARBARA   That man — we should warn him.

KEPLER   Hello, sir. (*moving closer*) Sir....He doesn't answer.

BARBARA	Perhaps he's deaf.
KEPLER	(*to the man*) There are soldiers on the road. (*pausing*) He doesn't answer.
BARBARA	Perhaps he's Catholic.
KEPLER	Were you expelled from the town also?
MAN	Yes.
KEPLER	Are you Lutheran?
MAN	No.
KEPLER	Catholic?
MAN	No.
KEPLER	Do you believe in the selling of indulgences?
MAN	I believe in shouting.
KEPLER	What?
MAN	(*at the top of his lungs*) Lord!
KEPLER	Quiet! The soldiers will come!
MAN	Great shouts make heaven take notice.
KEPLER	That's impossible.
MAN	Why?
KEPLER	Heaven is too far away.
MAN	How do you know?
KEPLER	I calculated it.
MAN	Lord!
KEPLER	Sh!

The man is shaken by a spasm.

MAN   The lord enjoys a good jerk as well.

BARBARA   He's dying.

MAN   One night, two days ago, I awoke and found my
                mouth filled with loud laughter. Since then I
                have spread the good news.

BARBARA   Look on his neck. There are boils.

MAN   The least little whisper — God marks it down.
                Every leaf that falls from the trees — God hears.
                Think of all the trees.

BARBARA   (*pulling at* KEPLER) Come away — he's
                infected.

MAN   Lord! Help me!

BARBARA   Please.

MAN   Lord! Help me!

Act One, Scene Five

> JEPP *crouches, gnawing a bone.*
> KEPLER *calls offstage.*

KEPLER   Hello?

> JEPP *hides under a table.* KEPLER *and*
> BARBARA *enter.*

BARBARA   There's no one here. The castle is deserted.

KEPLER   It's dark.

BARBARA   All the windows are covered.

> JEPP *moves under the table.*

BARBARA   There's someone under the table.

KEPLER   Hello. Can you help us? Is this the castle of the Stars?

BARBARA   You needn't be afraid of us. You can come out.

JEPP   This is my home.

BARBARA   Why do you live under a table?

JEPP   Why do you live under the sky?

BARBARA   This is a strange welcome.

KEPLER	I am Johannes Kepler. I am an astronomer.
BARBARA	He doesn't know you.
KEPLER	Where is your master?
JEPP	Asleep.
KEPLER	The sun is up seven hours.
JEPP	He keeps to his bed by day. Like a bat.
KEPLER	This must be the place

> BARBARA *clutches her stomach.*

KEPLER	Are you alright?
BARBARA	I must lie down soon.
KEPLER	Perhaps you could show us to our quarters. My wife is pregnant. She has given birth prematurely before.
JEPP	A bitch in a hurry gives blind pups.

> KEPLER *kicks at* JEPP. *Voices off.*

BARBARA	Someone's coming.
KEPLER	It may be Brahe. Our life is in his hands. He's very tempermental. Don't mention his nose.
BARBARA	His nose?

> BRAHE *enters with three men in time to hear "His nose." He has a gold nose. He wears a great fur coat.*

KEPLER	Great Astronomer!
BRAHE	Who are you?
KEPLER	Johannes Kepler.

BRAHE	Kepler?
KEPLER	You must excuse our appearance. We had a difficult journey.
BRAHE	I can see that.
KEPLER	This is my wife Barbara.
EISLER	She makes a lovely addition to our circle.
KEPLER	Thank you.
EISLER	The praise was meant for her, not you.
	Everyone laughs.
BRAHE	Quiet! These are my assistants Bruno, Eisler, and Longomontanous.
KEPLER	I am happy to meet you
BRAHE	I expect you are tired.
BARBARA	Yes.
KEPLER	Did you receive my correspondence?
BRAHE	It arrived last Friday. Your room is last along that hall.
KEPLER	Have you had time to read my book?
BRAHE	Yes. You should rest.
BARBARA	Come.
KEPLER	I am never too tired for a scientific discussion.
BRAHE	Dinner is at six. We will discuss your work then. We are expecting a conjunction of Jupiter and Mars tonight if you wish to observe it.

KEPLER   Thank you. You were my only hope. I seek no other glory than to be your assistant.

BRAHE   You are too polite.

KEPLER   Your fame exceeds the ancients as the sun exceeds the lesser stars. Wherever men speak of intelligence your name is invoked.

BRAHE   You do me too much honour.

KEPLER   I only express what is the case.

BRAHE   Yes, I suppose so.

KEPLER   And you sir, have you had time to digest my theory?

BRAHE   About the five perfect solids?

KEPLER   Yes.

BRAHE   I have.

KEPLER   I would be honoured by your opinion of my ideas.

BRAHE   I attribute them to youth. You show some promise but are hardly a scientist.

> JEPP *laughs under the table.* KEPLER *looks at* LONGOMONTANUS *who is writing furiously.*

KEPLER   What are you writing sir?

LONGOMONT   We record all of the Imperial Mathematician's conversations for posterity.

KEPLER   I maintain my ideas are excellent.

BRAHE   I'm afraid you're wrong.

KEPLER   In what way?

BRAHE	You invent where you should describe.
KEPLER	The creator is the inventor. I am merely his poor secretary, living by his charity.
BRAHE	Your poverty is excuseable. But your ideas aren't.
	Everyone laughs.
KEPLER	They are not my ideas.
BRAHE	Whose then?
KEPLER	The one who spoke to me in a flash of inspiration.
BRAHE	You must have misheard him.
KEPLER	He speaks in the clear and unambiguous language of mathematics. Without it we are mere stuttering fools.
BRAHE	The gift of speech is not enough for our work. Nature is like a woman. Few know how to woo her. You must observe her a long time and learn to ask the right questions.
KEPLER	Maestlin called me the greatest geometer in Europe!
JEPP	And the worst astronomer.
KEPLER	Idiot!
BRAHE	We are not pure intelligences. We cannot know things by the unaided strength of our minds. We need our eyes. I'll teach you to use yours.
KEPLER	I want nothing to do with you sir!
BRAHE	Where can you go? The Emperor has guaranteed your well being. This is the only place you are safe.

KEPLER   The Emperor may change his mind.

BRAHE   The Emperor cares nothing for religion. He cares about the stars.

KEPLER   Then he will be sorry you have driven me away.

KEPLER turns to go.

BARBARA   Humble yourself!

KEPLER   No!

KEPLER begins to exit. BARBARA follows

BRAHE   Where's my ointment?

EISLER hands BRAHE some oil which he rubs on his nose.

BRAHE   I'm not feeling well today doctor.

KEPLER stops.

BRAHE   The gall has gone to my head.

KEPLER   Gall?

EISLER   You should eat more walnuts.

BRAHE   You doctors are all the same. You can describe every illness down to the last cyst or dysfunction. You have a name for everything. But when it comes to producing a cure, all you can do is talk. You try to defeat sickness by holding up a mirror to it. The walnut cures headaches because it looks like a brain. Do you think God is that simple? That he put the sign of everything on its surface?

EISLER   The creator did not wish anything he made for our benefit to remain hidden.

BRAHE Yes — but he's not a fool. You play an endless game of resemblances.

LONGOMONT You're right. We need a mechanical principle that goes deeper than that. I have discovered such a principle.

BRAHE Which is?

LONGOMONT The Law of Suction.

BRAHE Suction?

LONGOMONT When the dog barks, the ear sucks it up, the eye sucks up light, the lungs air and the female organ the male.

JEPP And the mouth food

Everyone laughs.

LONGOMONT My law is too far reaching for you, shitbreaches. But little by little the advancing generations will understand its true value. In all the cosmos there is nothing but suction!

BRUNO No!

LONGOMONT All movement is caused by suction!

BRUNO All motions strive to go straight. Until they are prevented. In all the cosmos there is nothing but straightflying! Nothing else ever happens at all!

LONGOMONT Suction!

BRUNO Straightflying!

LONGOMONT Suction!

BRUNO Straightflying!

BRUNO *jumps on*
LONGOMONTANUS *and pulls a knife.*
BRAHE *tries to restrain him.*

BRAHE   Gentlemen! We are the greatest minds in Europe.
We can settle our disputes peacefully.

JEPP   You could have a duel.

BRAHE   (*kicking at* JEPP) Dog!

KEPLER   This is not an observatory — it's a madhouse.
They know nothing here.

EISLER *pulls* BRUNO *aside.* BRAHE
turns to LONGOMONTANUS.

BRAHE   (*shaking him*) Haven't you anything better to do?
You promised to have the orbit of Mars today.

LONGOMONT   The calculations are very difficult. And you
haven't given me enough data.

BRAHE   You've been working on it for eight years!

KEPLER   (*to himself*) I could solve it in eight days.

BRAHE   Fine. The problem is yours. (*to*
LONGOMONTANUS) I assign you the moon.

LONGOMONT   The moon! It's a scandal!

BRAHE   We have a new member of our circle gentlemen.
Let him be an inspiration to us all. In eight days
he will lay the foundation of a new universe.

LONGOMONT   Ha!

Act One, Scene Six

> BARBARA *stands in darkness.* EISLER
> *crosses downstage.*

BARBARA   Good evening doctor.

EISLER   Oh...hello.

BARBARA   I couldn't sleep, so I decided to explore the castle. What are you hiding under your coat?

EISLER   Nothing.

> *A bone drops on the floor.*

BARBARA   What have you done?

EISLER   It's nothing. Sh!

> *Another bone drops as he tries to pick up the first.* BARBARA *screams.*

EISLER   Please!

BARBARA   It's black!

EISLER   It's from a woman who was burned. If anyone comes delay them.

BARBARA   No, please...

> EISLER *exits and returns shortly.*

EISLER   They'll be safe for now.

BARBARA   You should throw them from the walls.

EISLER   I walked five miles for them. The Inquisitor is detained at a town near here.

BARBARA   Detained?

EISLER   By witches.

BARBARA   He's coming here?

EISLER   Yes.

BARBARA   What for?

EISLER   You needn't be afraid. He's something of a scientist himself. Though not when it comes to witches.

BARBARA   Why did you risk your life for the bones?

EISLER   I'm drawing an anatomy.

BARBARA   It would be safer to consult the works of Galen.

EISLER   Galen is inaccurate. He put men together from the parts of pigs and monkeys. They didn't allow dissections in his day either.

BARBARA   Aren't you afraid?

EISLER   Yes...At the university I unearthed the corpses of prostitutes. I'd have myself locked out of the city at night to gather the parts of criminals. One murderer has taught me more than all my professors.

BARBARA   You scientists are indecent. Longomontanus has asked me if he can weigh my food and then my excrement.

EISLER   We are forced to look for knowledge wherever it lies. Up there or below. (*moving closer*) Where is your husband?

BARBARA   In the kitchen. Cutting vegetables.

EISLER   He's cooking? At midnight?

BARBARA   He's studying their shapes.

EISLER   Why isn't he watching the sky?

BARBARA   It's too cold.

EISLER   He's not well suited for the work.

BARBARA   He's always been frail.

EISLER   You have little in common.

BARBARA   Love isn't always a matter of temporal affinities.

                Pause.

EISLER   Has he solved the orbit of Mars?

BARBARA   Not yet.

EISLER   He has only two days left.

BARBARA   He's very clever. Once he saw some men selling wine and told them a way of measuring the volume of the barrels. Last February he predicted a storm to the hour. Now when the people of our town see the sky darkening they say it's that Kepler coming. His mind is always among the stars.

EISLER   My heaven is much closer. And when I ask a question, the answer drops in my lap.

                Pause.

BARBARA   Your questions are too subtle for my knowledge.

EISLER	I want you.
BARBARA	I'm in no condition.
EISLER	Don't you want any joy from life?
BARBARA	Pleasure is the greatest incitement to evil.
EISLER	(*taking her hand*) So I've heard. D'you know that man is the only animal that cries? He cries the moment of birth but is considered a genius if he laughs within forty days.

JEPP *laughs under the table.*

EISLER	That damn dwarf. He sees everything. My bones!

EISLER *exits.*

BARBARA	You spend all your hours under that table.
JEPP	You spend as many in your room.

Pause.

BARBARA	I go there to meditate.
JEPP	Are you weak?
BARBARA	No. I prefer it there.
JEPP	You're always reading the Book of Martyrs.
BARBARA	Yes.
JEPP	Have you noticed that most of them are women?
BARBARA	Yes.
JEPP	How do you account for that?
BARBARA	God wishes to show that he can make something out of nothing.

JEPP   (*laughing*)You're very clever.

BARBARA   My husband is clever. I have no understanding of
                heavenly things.

JEPP   Neither does your husband. He'll never understand
                the motions of Mars.

BARBARA   Why not?

JEPP   Because a devil pushes it about at will.

BARBARA   Others consider him an authority.

JEPP   I am not like others. This form is not in Adam's
                likeness or in Eve's. I was sired by a witch.

BARBARA   There are no witches.

                                JEPP *laughs.*

BARBARA   Why do you laugh?

JEPP   Few have seen them. I am small so they are not
                afraid of me.

BARBARA   Where have you seen them?

JEPP   In the fields at night. I could take you.

BARBARA   I have no desire to see them.

                                Pause.

BARBARA   What do they do?

JEPP   Dance in a ring. A devil sits in the middle.
                Afterwards they lie together — men and women.

BARBARA   Do you lie with them?

JEPP   The thought of a naked woman makes me ill.

BARBARA   Do they fly?

JEPP	Yes. I could show you.
BARBARA	No. I have no need of spells. My books are my ladders.

Pause.

BARBARA	How do they fly?

JEPP *hands her a small phial.*

BARBARA	What's this?
JEPP	An ointment.
BARBARA	What for?
JEPP	Rub it on your thighs. At night. Sitting by a window.

Pause. BARBARA *examines the phial.*

BARBARA	How much?
JEPF	Depends on how strong you are.
BARBARA	Have you used it?
JEPP	Yes.
BARBARA	And?
JEPP	It's only for women.

BARBARA *laughs.*

JEPP	I could show you.

Pause.

BARBARA	Perhaps. It's late. I must go to my room.

Act One, Scene Seven

> KEPLER *stands looking into a cradle.*
> BARBARA *has been crying.*

BARBARA   Leave him. Don't look anymore.

KEPLER   I can't stop.

> *Pause.*

KEPLER   When a painter creates a monster he uses the
forms he observes in nature. From a few parts and
colours all the horrors of the world are formed.

> *Pause.*

KEPLER   His nose is a pig's. His genitals look like boiled
turtle shells. The doctor says it comes from
eating too many turtles.

> *Pause.*

KEPLER   I'm not sure I believe him. But we must be
careful of over indulgence in anything.

BARBARA   I have tried to live a blameless life.

> *Pause.*

BARBARA   Come away.

> *Pause.*

BARBARA   You must sleep.

KEPLER   When I lie down everything spins.

BARBARA   You should rest.

KEPLER   I can't. Tycho has told me I must write a
               pamphlet defending his system. He's too old to
               build anything new. If I prove the earth moves
               his life's work will be destroyed.

                              Pause.

BARBARA   (*looking into the cradle*) Does the earth need an
               angel to keep it in motion?

KEPLER   God has no need of spirits. There's a force that
               emanates from the sun and moves the planets.

BARBARA   A force?

KEPLER   Like an invisible broom.

BARBARA   That's hardly better than an angel.

KEPLER   The world is a clock driven by physical causes.

BARBARA   If God set it in motion then it would run
               perfectly.

KEPLER   Yes.

BARBARA   No need for repairs.

KEPLER   Yes.

BARBARA   So what does he do?

KEPLER   Do?

BARBARA   After he winds his clock. It would run by itself.
               Are you saying God is idle?

KEPLER   God could never be idle.

BARBARA   Then what does he do?

                Pause.

KEPLER   These questions are too subtle for your
                intelligence.

BARBARA   Yes. I wish I could understand. Why is he so
                misshapen?

                BARBARA *takes the baby from the
                cradle.*

BARBARA   Perhaps the doctor is right. I may be to blame.

KEPLER   The doctor is mistaken. You should stay away
                from him.

BARBARA   He knows how to use his eyes.

KEPLER   He relies too much on them. He's misled by
                analogies.

BARBARA   He's drawn a correct picture of the body.

                KEPLER *draws a circle on the floor.*

KEPLER   D'you see this? Look at it closely. What do you
                see?

BARBARA   I see a circle.

KEPLER   But not with your eyes.

BARBARA   With what then?

KEPLER   When I draw a circle the lines are never perfectly
                round. Perfect roundness and perfect straightness
                are only in our minds. We never see them in this
                world. The real circle is in your mind. We see
                with our minds.

                BARBARA *sings softly to the baby.*

KEPLER   (*looking at the circle*) Of all the figures it is the
                most beautiful, for every part is equidistant from
                the centre. Its idea was with God before the
                creation. It is his essence. There is a higher kind
                of knowledge unmixed with colours, sounds or
                smells. If we lost our eyes and ears and noses we
                would perceive only that.

                            Pause.

BARABARA   Then Tycho is lucky to have lost his nose.

KEPLER   Stop it!

                        KEPLER *takes the baby.*

BARABARA   Where are you going?

KEPLER   To bury our son.

BARBARA   Dig a deep grave. So he won't be disturbed.

KEPLER   We will try again. I will consult my charts. I
                will find a good date for us to start.

BARBARA   Yes.

Act One, Scene Eight

	KEPLER *looks through the sights of a quadrant.* BRAHE *and his assistants stand nearby.*
BRAHE	Point the arm at Mars. Then record the angle in this book. No, like this. You're shaking!
KEPLER	This morning my wife forced me to bathe my entire body in hot water. The heat has constricted my bowels and given me a fever.
BRAHE	I'll do it.
	KEPLER stands aside.
LONGOMONT	Have you solved the orbit of Mars?
KEPLER	No.
LONGOMONT	It's been seven months.
JEPP	And as many baths.
LONGOMONT	Have you noticed that Mars sometimes stands still and sometimes appears to move backwards?
KEPLER	Yes.
LONGOMONT	How do you account for these motions?
KEPLER	I am approaching a solution.

LONGOMONT   D'you know of Rheticus?

KEPLER   Yes.

LONGOMONT   He was a great genius. He went mad working on that problem. They found him one night with great bruises on his face and head. He said an angel had seized him by the hair and banged him against the walls and ceiling shouting — These are the motions of Mars!

Everyone laughs, except for KEPLER.

KEPLER   That is as it should be.

LONGOMONT   Why?

KEPLER   The great problems mercilessly reject all who are not destined to solve them.

LONGOMONT   Mars will defeat you too! No simple shape will explain its orbit.

BRUNO   He thinks there are brooms that sweep the sky.

LONGOMONT   To clean up his mess — the five heavenly solids.

BRAHE   Gentlemen, please.

BRAHE *continues with his observations.*

KEPLER   It's cold tonight.

LONGOMONT   Perhaps you would rather be in the kitchen.

KEPLER   Listen, do you hear a noise?

LONGOMONT   What kind of noise?

KEPPLER   Music. From the sky.

LONGOMONT   He *is* mad. He thinks he's Pythagoras.

KEPLER   You need a purified ear.

BRUNO   Perhaps you could sing for us.

JEPP   You need a purified mouth.

LONGOMONT   His wife sings better.

BRUNO   Where is she?

JEPP   With the doctor.

BRUNO   He'll give her something to make strong children.

                    They all laugh.

BRAHE   Gentlemen, please!

KEPLER   The fate of our children is not determined here on earth.

LONGOMONT   Oh?

KEPLER   The planets, the angles at which they subdivide the sphere, that's what's important, not your astrology of rams and scorpions.

JEPP   What angle resulted in my birth?

LONGOMONT   (*making an angle with his hand and comparing it to* JEPP) Forty five degrees I would think.

                    They laugh. BRAHE *approaches* KEPLER.

BRAHE   You haven't been watching! How will you carry on my work? You have no evidence. You must give up your fantasies. Trust your eyes. If the earth moved we'd all be left behind!

                    Pause.

BRAHE   We must increase our efforts. Our work is going
                            badly. The history of the world is written in the
                            night sky if we could read it. We could improve
                            man's condition beyond imagining.
                            Longomontanus you and Bruno stay here. Kepler
                            and I will work on the east tower.

                                  BRAHE *exits with* KEPLER *and* JEPP.

LONGOMONT   Did you speak with the dwarf?

BRUNO   He won't help us. There's no way of getting
                            Brahe's data apart from killing him and taking the
                            key.

LONGOMONT   He's getting old. Perhaps he'll die soon.

BRUNO   Kepler would still have a claim.

LONGOMONT   We must make sure he leaves the castle.

BRUNO   (*looking through the instrument*) We may soon
                            have some help in that — Look, smoke!

LONGOMONT   They're burning someone in the village.

                                  Pause.

LONGOMONT   It's a clear night. The smoke rises to heaven with
                            our prayers.

BRUNO   The Inquisitor is here.

Act One, Scene Nine

	KEPLER *hides behind a pillar.* BRAHE *enters.*
KEPLER	Tycho.
BRAHE	Yes?
KEPLER	I must speak with you.
BRAHE	Why are you hiding?
KEPLER	They say the Emperor has gone mad.
BRAHE	The Emperor has always been mad.
KEPLER	He's a prisoner in Prague.
BRAHE	Yes.
KEPLER	His brother will succeed him. It was Frederick who expelled us from Gratz. If he comes to the throne there will be a war on the Lutherans.
BRAHE	You'll be safe here. Keep sending him your horoscopes. Even Frederick craves reassurance from the stars. We astronomers have more power than you think. We are above the quicksands of war and religion.
KEPLER	Why has he sent the Inquisitor?

BRAHE	Merely a visit.
KEPLER	(*seeing a soldier coming*) It's too much like Gratz.
SOLDIER	Johannes Kepler?
KEPLER	Yes?
SOLDIER	The Inquisitor wishes to see you.
KEPLER	Where is he?
SOLDIER	On his way.
BRAHE	I have work to do.

> BRAHE *exits. The* INQUISITOR *enters riding a primitive tricycle with a table mounted on it. The table is covered with manuscripts which the* INQUISITOR *reads as he pedals. He almost runs into* KEPLER.

REMY	Johannes Kepler?
KEPLER	Yes.
REMY	At last! I've been waiting to meet you. It's an honour.
KEPLER	Thank you.
REMY	I've heard the most wondrous things about your astrological talents. You predicted last year's long winter. And the war with the Turks.
KEPLER	Yes.
REMY	You must teach me how you do it.
KEPLER	It's not very difficult.

> REMY *laughs.*

KEPLER   No, really...all you need is a ruler and compass.
              It has to do with the science of angles, geometry.

REMY   You're a brilliant man.

KEPLER   Oh...it's nothing really.

REMY   We're very similar.

                        Pause.

REMY   D'you know what they call me?

KEPLER   No.

REMY   The marvel of Europe!

KEPLER   Really?

REMY   D'you know how old I am?

KEPLER   No.

REMY   Guess.

KEPLER   Nineteen?

REMY   (*disappointed*) Yes.

KEPLER   It's amazing.

REMY   My book on Seneca has over seventeen hundred
              references. I've taught myself to speak nine
              languages. I've read all the works of the
              philosophers. D'you know how I accomplished
              all this?

KEPLER   No.

REMY   By means of my inventions. This vehicle, for
              instance, allows me to navigate the stacks of a
              large library at an average speed of twelve miles
              an hour. In one day I can accomplish fifty per-
              cent more than the most energetic monk can in

REMY   (*continued*) two. By the age of thirty I hope to know as much as anyone who ever lived.

KEPLER   It's astonishing.

REMY   You'll not find me close-minded. Science, I have decided, is a way of worship. I am not like my fellows. I enjoy a good disputation. God has intended everything for our investigation.

KEPLER   Yes.

REMY   Unfortunately there are many interruptions. The number of witches is marvelously increased within this realm. In one village alone this year we had to burn two hundred. We flogged the children in front of their mother's fires. That vermin is multiplying upon the land like caterpillars in a garden. I wish they had one body, so we could burn them all at once — in one fire. (*pausing*) How many of your children have died?

KEPLER   Three.

REMY   That's a lot.

KEPLER   Yes.

REMY   You should be careful. There are malign influences in your house. I would keep a close watch on your wife. Learn the signs of witchcraft. Where is your wife?

KEPLER   In her room.

REMY   Good. It will be dark soon. Women are like frogs — they go open mouthed for the lure of things that do not concern them. There are places close to here where a thousand gather at once. They fly from all over Europe to conduct their orgies. I have evidence of this, from people who have seen it.

Pause.

REMY	We will dicuss this when I have time. I would like to hear your opinions.
KEPLER	Yes.
REMY	You must prepare me a horoscope...and teach me how to prognosticate.
KEPLER	Yes.
REMY	Goodbye (*turning to go*) Is something the matter?

Pause.

KEPLER	I think we should use our studies to increase the harmony in the world.
REMY	That's obvious. Is that all?
KEPLER	Yes.
REMY	Goodbye then.

REMY *turns and rides off.*

Act Two, Scene One

KEPLER *stands on the roof of the castle looking at the sky.* BARBARA *enters.*

BARBARA   I've been looking for you.

Pause.

BARBARA   Am I disturbing you?

KEPLER   No.

Pause.

BARBARA   It's a clear night. Why is no one working?

KEPLER   Tycho is still locked in his room. I can only speak to him through the door.

BARBARA   When will he come out?

KEPLER   No one knows. His assistants are all drunk. That dwarf crouches under the table at meals. And I must suffer endless discussions with the Inquisitor.

BARBARA   He scares me. Tonight, at dinner, he couldn't keep his eyes off my neck. D'you suppose it's true...that witches gather at night?

KEPLER   It's nonsense.

Pause.

BARBARA   Last night, when you were asleep, I felt your hand groping to see if I was there.

KEPLER   Listen? D'you hear it?

BARBARA   What?

KEPLER   Singing.

BARBARA   Yes...It's coming from the stairs.

> *The singing grows louder.*
> LONGOMONTANUS *and* BRUNO
> *stumble on drunk.*
> LONGOMONTANUS *wears a tail and beats on a blackened skull.* BRUNO *dances behind him, occassionally lifting his tail and kissing him on the ass.*

LONGOMONT   (*to* BRUNO) Here's a dish for the devil! (*lifting his tail and presenting his backside for* BARBARA *to kiss*)

BARBARA   Get away!

BRUNO   She prefers the doctor.

BARBARA   Where did you find that skull?

LONGOMONT   Under your pillow.

BRUNO   (*pointing*) Look, a fire.

LONGOMONT   In that forest a thousand women are waiting for us!

BRUNO   We should fly to them.

LONGOMONT   You first.

BRUNO   I forgot my broomstick.

LONGOMONT   Perhaps Kepler has one.

BRUNO   If he does he should fly north, like a good Lutheran.

LONGOMONT   D'you know of Baron Von Demback?

BRUNO   No.

LONGOMONT   His Lutheran peasants kicked him out. He returned with the Inquisitor. Soon the village square looked like a little forest after a fire.

BRUNO   Look, the moon is rising!

LONGOMONT   We must get to our women.

BRUNO   (*to* BARBARA) Don't keep us waiting.

> BRUNO *and* LOMGOMONTANUS *exit.* JEPP *enters unseen.*

KEPLER   I cannot stay here any longer. We must leave.

BARBARA   How will you work without Tycho's data?

KEPLER   I can't. But it's not safe here.

BARBARA   Where will we go?

JEPP   Tycho wants you.

KEPLER   Where?

JEPP   In his room.

KEPLER   Tell him I'm coming.

> JEPP *exits.*

KEPLER   I'll ask him for a letter recommending me. We'll find a university.

BARBARA   Alright.

KEPLER   We must leave quickly. There's going to be a
war. Worse than any we've seen. It will engulf
the world. No one knows what to believe. The
factions have torn the truth in pieces between
them.

Act Two, Scene Two

> BRAHE *sits in a chair examining a tiny*
> *model of the universe.* JEPP *enters.*

BRAHE   Did you talk with Kepler?

JEPP   Yes.

BRAHE   What did he say?

JEPP   He's leaving you.

BRAHE   Leaving me?

> *Pause.*

BRAHE   What are the others doing?

JEPP   Drinking.

BRAHE   The whole enterprise is collapsing. My life's
work. Bring me my ledger.

JEPP   Why should I serve you?

BRAHE   I'm ill.

> JEPP *brings him the ledger.* BRAHE
> *writes.*

JEPP   What are you writing?

BRAHE	A letter to the Emperor. You must see that Kepler gets it.
JEPP	Why?
BRAHE	I've been good to you haven't I?
JEPP	No.

Pause.

BRAHE	I hope you'll remember me kindly.
JEPP	No one will remember Tycho Brahe.
BRAHE	I'm more famous than the Pope. I'm the most famous man on earth.
JEPP	There are many more famous.
BRAHE	Who?
JEPP	Ptolemy, Aristotle, Galen.
BRAHE	They're all dead.
JEPP	So are you. Your reputation won't outlast your instruments.
BRAHE	Get out!

> BRAHE *throws the model of the universe at* JEPP, *who flees as* KEPLER *enters.*

BRAHE	Kepler — I didn't think you were coming.
KEPELR	Why do you keep that dwarf?
BRAHE	He humbles me.

Pause.

BRAHE	Thank you for coming. I'm sorry to take you away from your work.
KEPLER	I cannot write another pamphlet.
BRAHE	That's not why I asked you here.
KEPLER	Your system is full of flaws. You cannot keep the earth at the centre. It will never work. And my own research is going badly. It's very difficult when you give me so little data. The noise of the household is intolerable. I have decided....What's the matter? Why are you crying?
BRAHE	I miss my elk.
KEPLER	Your elk?

Pause.

KEPLER	Where is he?
BRAHE	Dead.

Pause.

KEPLER	How did he die?
BRAHE	Of drink. He fell down some stairs.

Pause.

KEPLER	I won't ask how that happened.
BRAHE	He used to eat from my hand. We understood each other.

Pause.

BRAHE	There's a little light we're born with. We lose it as we grow older.

Pause.

BRAHE   I know what's coming. I know it exactly — but I
                 don't tell others. They might think I was mad.
                 So I watch the stars. Even though I don't believe
                 in them.

KEPLER   You don't believe in them?

BRAHE   No.

KEPLER   You have accomplished more than all the
                 astronomers put together. They thought that
                 nothing could change beyond the sphere of the
                 moon. Thanks to your observations we will one
                 day understand the movement of the stars.

BRAHE   It's true that I discovered a new star. I owe
                 everything to that. Tycho's star. It burned
                 brighter than all the rest for two years then
                 disappeared. Some say I'm becoming luminous
                 myself. Starting with my nose. When I die I'm
                 going to become part of the firmament. I've
                 already picked out the spot. If you see a new star
                 to the right of Cassiopeia it'll be me. But they'll
                 call it Kepler's star.

KEPLER   Why are you so morbid tonight?

BRAHE   Whatever questions we put to nature, we get the
                 same answer back; remind yourself of the day
                 you will meet your end.

KEPLER   You need a good night's sleep.

BRAHE   I'm dying.

KEPLER   Nonsense.

BRAHE   Here, feel my forehead.

KEPLER   It's a little hot.

BRAHE   I was a guest at Baron Rosenburg's the other night. I had been drinking excessively and was seated beside that bore Kraus. He talked for two hours about his library. I held back my water beyond the bounds of courtesy. When I arrived home I could scarcely piss. Since then I've been feverish and passed water only with the greatest pain.

KEPLER   I'll get Eisler.

BRAHE   No. They're all quacks and charlatans.

KEPLER   Let me help you to bed.

BRAHE   You're the only one I trust. Don't let my work fall into their hands.You must continue to defend my system. We will be the co-founders of a new universe.

KEPLER   Stand up.

BRAHE   There's a letter in my ledger. Take it to the Emperor. I've asked him to appoint you my successor.

KEPLER   Your successor?

BRAHE   Yes.

KEPLER   It won't be necessary. You'll be fine tomorrow.

BRAHE   Promise me.

KEPLER   Yes, yes.

BRAHE   You must believe in my ideas. Don't let me seem to have lived in vain.

KEPLER   Yes...come to bed.

> KEPLER *helps* BRAHE *stand.* BRAHE *groans and clutches his groin.*

BRAHE   I'm dying.

KEPLER   You're not.

BRAHE   Of politeness.

>   BRAHE *stumbles into* KEPLER's
>   *arms.*

Act Two, Scene Three

> BARBARA *stands looking at the stars.*
> REMY *enters.*

REMY   You're up late.

BARBARA   I was looking for my husband.

REMY   Did you find him.

BARBARA   Yes. He's with Tycho.

> BARBARA *begins to exit.*

REMY   Where are you going?

BARBARA   To my room. I neglected my prayers after dinner.

REMY   What is the book you're carrying?

BARBARA   The Bible.

REMY   You have another book.

BARBARA   The Ship of Assured Safety.

REMY   No — a book you write in.

BARBARA   I keep a diary for my daughter.

REMY   You have no daughter.

BARBARA I will.

      Pause.

REMY   You must avoid passionate coitus. The heat
      curdles the matter. That is the cause of the death
      of your children.You should seek union with the
      window open.

      Pause.

BARBARA You're very young.

REMY   Nineteen.

      Pause.

REMY   Do I frighten you?

BARBARA No.

      REMY *holds up a blackened bone.*

REMY   I found this tonight. It has earth on it. It's from a
      woman who was burned. The astronomers cannot
      see what is right under their noses.

      Pause.

REMY   Have you ever spoken to a witch?

BARBARA I don't believe in witches.

REMY   It's a sin not to believe in witches.

      Pause.

BARBARA I'm sorry. I have tried to live a virtuous life. But
      it's hard to know what to believe. I live with the
      wisest men in Europe. Each says he knows the
      truth but none can agree.

REMY

You're a simple woman. Remember, the devil can trick the senses and darken even the most brilliant mind. In a dark time few can see the truth. I have gathered evidence of witchcraft from across Europe. You must be careful. Heretics are those who remain obstinate in error. Believers are those who put their faith in the errors of heretics. And concealers are those who know heretics and do not denounce them.

Pause.

BARBARA

Is it true witches fly?

REMY

Yes. I have extracted confessions from hundreds of women. Most have flown. Even women of seventy years.

BARBARA

How do they fly?

REMY

Sometimes on the back of an incubus, sometimes a broom. Some use an ointment. (*laughing*) One woman....But you shouldn't think too much on these things — remember, the fire here cannot last more than an hour. But in hell it is eternal.

Pause.

REMY

I don't expect people's praise for what I do. That would be like the eye expecting a reward for seeing. I begin each day by telling myself — today I will meet with interference, ingratitude, ill-will and selfishness. But all that is merely due to the offender's ignorance of good and evil. God has endured man's ignorance for centuries. I only have to put up with it for a few decades. So I try to remain cheerful.

BARBARA

You've had a difficult life.

REMY

Yes. How lucky I am that it has left me with no bitterness.

Pause.

BARBARA   Thank you for your advice. It's late. I must go to my room.

BARBARA *turns to go.*

REMY   There are many signs of witchcraft in the castle. When you are alone, act as if God can see you.

BARBARA   I will.

Act Two, Scene Four

BARBARA *lies slumped in a chair.*
KEPLER *enters with* EISLER.

KEPLER   In here, quickly...She's here.

EISLER *bends down and examines*
BARBARA.

KEPLER   Is she dead?

EISLER   No. She fainted.

EISLER   (*picking up a small phial*) Here's the cause.

KEPLER   What is it?

EISLER   An ointment. I've heard of women that use it. The nightshade sends them to sleep. They all dream the same dream.

KEPLER   What dream?

EISLER   Of flying.

BARBARA *groans.* JEPP *enters.*

KEPLER   She's waking.

EISLER   Yes. She'll be fine

KEPLER   Tomorrow I must go to the Emperor. Will you
          take care of her?

EISLER   The Emperor?

KEPLER   I have a letter from Tycho. He's asked me to save
          his data from the others.

JEPP   Tycho is dead.

KEPLER   What?

JEPP   I found him on the East tower. Looking at the
          stars.

KEPLER   (*beginning to exit*) I must hurry.

EISLER   Can you leave so suddenly? Have you no
          feelings?

KEPLER   Only one thing matters — Divine truth. It will
          be lost if I wait.

                    KEPLER *exits.* BARBARA *stands and
                    takes a few uncertain steps.*

EISLER   Did you fly?

Act Two, Scene Five

EISLER, REMY, *and* LONGOMONTANUS
*stand in front of a chair with screws attached to
its legs.and arms.*

EISLER   Do we have to go through with this?

REMY   You examined the body yourself. The penis was
obstructed.

EISLER   Yes — but he could have died from natural
causes.

REMY   The testicles of her child were shrivelled. There is
impotence throughout the land. And I have
stronger evidence.

EISLER   What is it?

A SOLDIER *leads* BARBARA *in.*

REMY   You will see with your own eyes...Put her in
there.

The SOLDIER *straps her into the
machine.*

LONGOMONT   How does the machine work?

REMY   The screws here and here crush the fingers, and
these, the shin bones.

BARBARA	My husband has gone to the Emperor. He'll have you burnt alive.
REMY	I am the Emperor's servant.
EISLER	Stop! Why must you put her in there? She's terrified.
REMY	If it weren't for the pain and fear the answers would be subjective. The machine ensures an objective answer.
LONGOMONT	I see.
REMY	This is proven by the consistency of the confessions I have extracted. Slowly a picture of the devil's activity across Europe is emerging. You have to learn to ask the right questions.
LONGOMONT	Show us.
REMY	(*to* BARBARA) How long have you had this wart?
EISLER	What's the point of that question?
REMY	Quiet. You shall see. How long have you had this wart?
BARBARA	I don't know.
REMY	When I came here five weeks ago your neck was spotless.
BARBARA	You pay so much attention to my neck?
REMY	The neck is where the incubus sucks. After several weeks the place becomes hardnened and impervious to pain.
EISLER	(*examining the spot*) It's a wart.
REMY	Prick it.

> REMY *hands* EISLER *a pin.* EISLER
> *pricks the spot.*

REMY   You see, it doesn't bleed. She felt nothing.

EISLER   It's very unusual.

REMY   Three days ago Longomontanus discovered a
skull in the East tower.

EISLER   A skull?

REMY   Since then I have made a thorough search of the
castle. (*taking some vegetables from his pocket*)
D'you recognize these?

BARBARA   Yes.

LONGOMONT What are they?

REMY   I found them in the kitchen. This cucumber
looks like the moon. This turnip has the crude
shape of the host.

LONGOMONT How did they get that way? Did they grow like
that?

REMY   A witches magic works by imitation. She carved
them.

> BARBARA *laughs.*

REMY   This is part of the witchcraft that killed Brahe.
How many of your children have died?

> *Pause.* REMY *tightens the screws.*
> BARBARA *screams.*

REMY   How many?

BARBARA   Three.

REMY   So many?

Pause.

REMY   You smear yourself with their fat and fornicate
                with the devil. When did the devil first come to
                you?

LONGOMONT   Have you slept with the devil?

                Pause.

REMY   Have you slept with the devil?

BARBARA   Yes. (*pausing*) We went to a graveyard. He
                begged my forgiveness — said he would just be a
                minute if I would wait. You see...he had to
                unearth a corpse. The priests are right — he can't
                father children without borrowed matter. He had
                to squeeze and squeeze the testicles of the corpse
                he found and even then — only a little drop came
                out. The matter had been underground so long,
                all it engendered was worms.

LONGOMONT   She's making fun of us.

REMY   No — her testimony is very similar to others I
                have heard.

                BARBARA *laughs.*

LONGOMONT   Ask her again.

REMY   (*tightening the screws*) Have you slept with the
                devil?

BARBARA   (*in pain*) Yes!

                REMY *loosens the screws.*

REMY   How many times?

BARBARA   I can't remember.

REMY   Did he come to you as a man?

BARBARA	No.
LONGOMONT	What's he like?
BARBARA	Like?
LONGOMONT	Yes.
BARBARA	He's not like anything. (*pausing*) You only know similarities. Your bones are rocks, your veins great rivers, your thoughts air, and your soul fire. But you're only a man. The devil knows more than similarities. (*pausing*) You could say the pulse beats in his veins the way the stars circle the sky...but that would be too little.
EISLER	She's raving...let her go.

> REMY *tightens the screws.* BARBARA *screams.*

REMY	What's he like?
BARBARA	I don't know.
LONGOMONT	They say his skin is freezing to the touch.
BARBARA	Yes — it's as cold as death.
REMY	Yes! That's right! That's what I've heard!
LONGOMONT	What's he like as a lover?
BARBARA	His touch gives neither pleasure nor pain.

> REMY *tightens the screws.*

BARBARA	God! Save me! Help me!
REMY	Now the fiend is speaking. Listen!
EISLER	She's bleeding.

REMY   That's enough. She has confessed. D'you
understand that a miracle has occured? From
under a cloud of appearances we have dragged the
devil. Lock him in a cell. We will burn him in
the morning.

Act Two, Scene Six

BARBARA *lies on a stone floor.*
KEPLER *and* JEPP *enter.* KEPLER
carries a bag over his shoulder.

KEPLER   We've come to the wrong place. There's no-one
here. I can't see.

JEPP   Sh!

KEPLER   We're lost.

JEPP   I know these cells. I've spent time here...There
she is.

KEPLER *approaches* BARBARA.

KEPLER   Is it true?...Her fingers are bloody. God what
have I done?

JEPP   We haven't time to talk.

KEPLER *bends to touch* BARBARA
who pulls away and is about to scream.
He puts his hand over her mouth.

KEPLER   It's me.

BARBARA   I dreamt they'd come to burn me.

KEPLER   We must hurry. There's a carriage waiting. Baron
Drieser has offered us his home. Can you walk?

BARBARA	Yes. Of course.

> KEPLER *helps* BARBARA *stand. She groans and falls.*

BARBARA	My leg is broken.

> KEPLER *puts down the bag and helps* BARBARA *up.*

BARABARA	What's in the bag?
KEPLER	Tycho's data.
BARBARA	(*laughing*)You needn't have come for me.
KEPLER	Quiet! (*starting to exit, leaving the bag*)
BARBARA	Please don't leave it here.

> KEPLER *exits.* JEPP *begins to exit then turns back and drags the bag behind him.*

Act Two, Scene Seven

> BARBARA *sits reading a prayer book.*
> *She closes her eyes and tries to pray.*
> KEPLER *calls from off.*

KEPLER   Barbara? Barbara?

KEPLER   (*entering*)Why didn't you answer me?

BARBARA   I didn't hear you.

> *Pause.*

KEPLER   Have you eaten today?

BARBARA   No.

KEPLER   I bought some bread. What are you reading?

BARBARA   Nothing.

> *Pause.*

KEPLER   The Baron is pleased with his horoscope. I have
                  asked him for more money. I will buy you a new
                  dress. You haven't even the convenience of a
                  small mirror.

BARBARA   I don't need to look at myself...I see fire
                  everywhere.

KEPLER   It's been four years! Can't you forget? (*pausing*)
                  I'm sorry...Where's our daughter?

BARBARA	With Anya.
KEPLER	I have spoken with the Baron. He says we may have to take in soldiers. The Emperor's brother has raised an army. (*pausing*) D'you hear me?
BARBARA	Yes.
KEPLER	I could hardly sleep last night. My boils have returned. The stars are in the same position as at my birth. I may not have long to live.
BARBARA	Have you solved your problem?
KEPLER	I have been investigating light.
BARBARA	What have you discovered?
KEPLER	Nothing...Light has no substance and yet it acts and is acted upon. It has no existence in the space between objects, only when it strikes them. It has a present but no past. It is not like anything I understand.
	BARBARA *stands and limps towards him.*
BARBARA	You're wasting your time.
KEPLER	Please Barbara, I don't want to fight.
BARBARA	People will always fight. If not in armies then in pairs. Because they'll never agree. You say the sun stands still. That means we cannot trust our eyes. What will we trust?
KEPLER	It was a mistake to marry me. It has made us both miserable.
BARBARA	It's not your fault. The stars threw us together.

KEPLER	On my tenth birthday an eclipse occured as foretold. It seemed miraculous to me that we could know the future so accurately. That was my hope. (*pausing*) Longomontanus was right. The sky has defeated me.
BARBARA	(*looking out the window*) You must continue to work.
KEPLER	What do you see?
BARBARA	Fire.

Pause.

BARBARA	They've set the town on fire.
KEPLER	What? (*going to the window*) The war has started. We're trapped here.
BARBARA	The smoke rises to heaven...How far is heaven?

Act Two, Scene Eight

Sound of drums. KEPLER *is packing.*
He is visibly older. He picks up a
manuscript that has been partially burnt
and leafs through it, then puts it into a
bag. A SOLDIER *enters.*

SOLDIER   Kepler?

KEPLER   Yes?

SOLDIER   Don't you recognize me?

KEPLER   Thomas?

SOLDIER   That's right.

KEPLER   Where are you quartered now?

SOLDIER   On the other side of town — where the fighting
is worst...I have come to you for some advice.

KEPLER   What is it?

SOLDIER   I must choose a wife.

KEPLER   Who is the woman?

SOLDIER   There are three.

KEPLER   Three? Why have you come to me?

SOLDIER	I thought you might consult the stars.
KEPLER	You should trust yourself. I don't have time. I'm leaving tomorrow.
SOLDIER	I'm inclined to pick the second.
KEPLER	Then she must be the one.

> *Pause. The* SOLDIER *looks around the room.*

SOLDIER	I miss being here. We had many fine conversations.
KEPLER	Yes.
SOLDIER	Did you solve that problem you were working on?
KEPLER	Six months ago.
SOLDIER	Congratulations! Is there a book?
KEPLER	The printers I contracted burnt down during the fighting.
SOLDIER	Did you save the manuscript?
KEPLER	Yes. I have it packed away.
SOLDIER	You should guard it carefuly. Someone might steal it.

> KEPLER *laughs.*

SOLDIER	What's funny?
KEPLER	This morning I found out I arrived at my result by mistake. I made an error in my calculations which cancelled out two mistaken assumptions. I stumbled from confusion to confusion like someone sleeping.

SOLDIER	God must have been leading you.
KEPLER	He chose a strange path.

Sound of drums in the distance.

SOLDIER	Thank you for your advice. I have to get back to the wall.
KEPLER	I have a question for you.
SOLDIER	What is it?
KEPLER	When will the fighting start again?
SOLDIER	The men say a week. Perhaps this time the truce will last longer.
KEPLER	Thank you.

The SOLDIER *exits.* KEPLER *continues to pack.* LONGOMONTANUS *enters.*

LONGOMONT	Johannes Kepler?
KEPLER	Longomontanus!
LONGOMONT	The truce has allowed me to visit you.
KEPLER	This is a surprise.

LONGOMONTANUS *looks around the room.*

LONGOMONT	I can see your condition hasn't improved since you left Benatek so quickly.
KEPLER	They've quartered soldiers in my house because it's on the wall. I have a good view of the fighting. I can watch the lines of peasants cut down as they cross the fields.
LONGOMONT	How does your wife endure all this?

KEPLER   She died ten years ago.

                  Pause.

LONGOMONT   I'm sorry.

KEPLER   She contracted small pox from the soldiers. The
                  strain of the fighting was too much for her. I live
                  here with my daughter...How is Benatek?

LONGOMONT   After Tycho died many left. I have not been able
                  to keep the place going by myself. Most of the
                  instruments are rusted.

KEPLER   Poor Tycho. I have fond memories of him.

LONGOMONT   Yes — the dead get better with age.

                  Pause.

KEPLER   Why have you come?

LONGOMONT   I heard through a correspondent you have made
                  some discoveries.

KEPLER   Yes.

LONGOMONT   You had no right to take our data.

KEPLER   Tycho appointed me his successor.

LONGOMONT   What have you found?

KEPLER   I have struggled for more than a decade down
                  many blind alleys, misled by as many false
                  presuppositions. I have had to clear out the
                  stables of astronomy and am left with a single
                  cartload of dung.

LONGOMONT   Which is?

KEPLER   The planets move in ellipses, not circles. If you
                  draw a line between the sun and a planet it will
                  sweep out equal areas in equal times.

Pause.

LONGOMONT   Is that all?

KEPLER   Yes.

LONGOMONT   After all these years? It seems rather small.

KEPLER   But it's true. I've proven it geometrically.

LONGOMONT   Then you must sign my name to it.

KEPLER   Your name?

LONGOMONT   The Emperor has appointed me Imperial
Mathematican, with all rights to discoveries
made from Tycho's data. You must sign my
name as co-discoverer to any book publicising
these results or face imprisonment.

Pause.

KEPLER   Alright.

LONGOMONT   You agree?

KEPLER   It doesn't matter. I'm too old to fight.

LONGOMONT   When will the book be published?

KEPLER   The Emperor owes me six years back wages. I'm
destitute. The printing house I contracted was
burnt down by the soldiers. Unless you give me
some money the book will never see the light of
day.

LONGOMONT   How much do you need?

KEPLER   Three hundred Thalers.

LONGOMONT   Three hundred! I'm not a fool!

KEPLER   It's a small price to pay.

LONGOMONT	Your results are hardly that sensational.
KEPLER	You have more than enough money.
LONGOMONT	Not for that! (*pausing*). I'm dissappointed — you seemed to have so much promise. Your results are worthless. They are not a foundation but a swamp. God would be a shabby workman if what you say is true.
KEPLER	(*shaken*) Perhaps...I may be mistaken.
	KEPLER *rummages among some papers and hands a bundle to* LONGOMONTANUS.
KEPLER	Here's a copy of the data. I'm sorry I didn't send it to you .
LONGOMONT	I will tell the Emperor of your condition. Perhaps he will send you some money. The truce won't last long. The next round will be worse. The wars will continue until there is only a single faith left. You should go north.
KEPLER	Thank you.
	LONGOMONTANUS *turns to exit, stops.*
LONGOMONT	What is the name of your book?
KEPLER	*Harmony of the World.*
	LONGOMONTANUS *laughs and exits.* KEPLER *continues to pack. His daughter,* MARGARET, *enters.*
MARGARET	Who was that? He looked awful.
KEPLER	Someone I knew a long time ago.
MARGARET	Why did he come here?

KEPLER	For a visit.
MARGARET	I've found a coach to take us north tomorrow.
KEPLER	Good...are you packed?
MARGARET	Yes.

Pause.

MARGARET	Why are you so upset? What did he say to you?
KEPLER	Nothing.
MARGARET	I heard the soldiers talking when I was out. They said the war would start again soon.
KEPLER	They're only talking.
MARGARET	I'm not a child!

Pause.

KEPLER	Yes.
MARGARET	I'm almost sixteen.
KEPLER	Your mother would be proud of you. She wanted you more than anything.
MARGARET	Why do you never talk about her?
KEPLER	She had an unfortunate life.
MARGARET	Were you happy together?
KEPLER	No.

Pause.

MARGARET	I can hardly remember her. She used to throw me up in the air. She said she'd throw me right up into heaven. What was she like?

KEPLER   (*upset*) "Like" is a dangerous word. It has started
                  many wars. There are men who think the stars
                  are like immutable crystals and are willing to
                  burn everyone alive to prove it. And I have
                  wasted half my life because I thought that God
                  was like a circle. One day science will bring
                  about a different age, an age of reason, when
                  people will see things exactly with their minds,
                  not by analogy. When we know how things are
                  in themselves there will be no more reasons to
                  fight. How will anyone quarrel when God's
                  universal laws are discovered? Everyone will
                  agree.

                  Pause.

KEPLER   It's getting dark. You should be in bed.

MARGARET   Tomorrow we'll find a printer.

KEPLER   God had to wait six thousand years for someone
                  to understand his work. It would be fitting if I
                  had to wait as long.

MARGARET   People will remember you forever.

KEPLER   Our memories are still short. We are like light
                  passing through a room. Our past is invisible.

MARGARET   You used that word again.

KEPLER   What word?

MARGARET   Like.

                  Pause.

KEPLER   You should be in bed.

MARGARET   Can I look at the stars first? (*going to the
                  window*)

KEPLER   One day, if we can stop fighting over words, we will build ships with sails adjusted to the heavenly ether. There are heavenly bodies we may never see — beyond the visible stars.

MARGARET   What are they like? (*giggling*)

KEPLER   Like stars.

The End.